EXTRACTION OF CONFESSIONAL STATEMENTS

The suspects and the criminal justice in Nigeria.

Dairo Titilayo Abosede

DEDICATION

This book is dedicated to the Almighty God, the Giver of grace and strength, to the Holy Spirit my helper and comforter and to the oppressed whose rights were trampled upon and seek justice.

ACKNOWLEDGEMENTS

To the Almighty God, the giver of inspiration and direction to inquire knowledge and for given me grace to start and finish this book, to Him be praise now and forever.

I am also graceful specially to Prof. Adeniyi J. Olatunbosun, the Vice-Chancellor of the Kola Daisi University (KDU), Ibadan, Nigeria, for taking time out of his busy schedule to go through the manuscript and contents of this book. His useful and invaluable suggestions as well as encouragement has gone a long way in publishing this book.

I remain grateful to Dr Kazeem Olajide Olaniyan for the inspiration given towards publishing this book. I also appreciate my Lecturer; Dr M. Adigun for his immense contribution to this book. The duo of Dr Ademola Ojekunle and Kehinde Adegbite are well appreciated, my sincere appreciation also goes to my husband and children for their endurance and understanding in the course of writing the book, may God reward them abundantly.

PREFACE

Confessional statement is sufficient in law to establish the culpability of a defendant where proven at trial. Broad consensus in literature and available evidence indicate that the use of torture on suspects by the Nigerian police while obtaining their statements is rampant. Previous studies have focused mainly on torture by the Nigerian police as causes of high incidence of involuntary statements rejected at trial with little attention paid to the Evidence Act and the Administration of Criminal Justice Act. This study was therefore, designed to examine the laws on suspects' rights in Nigeria during interrogation with a view to ensure proper control, monitoring and the protection of the rights of suspects.

Provisions of the laws do not permit the use of torture and admissibility of unreliable statement; however, it exists in practice alongside psychological and other inducement methods. Implementation machineries are insufficient, administration of caution and other suspects' rights are qualified and unmonitored. Waiver of rights by suspects are unrecorded illiteracy and unavailability of funds limits access to legal practitioner of one's choice. Use of discretion promotes deliberate breach of suspects' right without punishment, save by way of exclusion during trial. Provisions on Audio/ visual interrogation' devices, storage, security and training are inadequate. Delay at trial, wrongful convictions, and soaring crime rate impugn the integrity of the CJS. In contrast, the U.K PACE Codes C, D, F, G and H, are detailed, well-structured with innovations for intimate, strip searches, conduct of interviews of suspects not under arrest, while violations of the Codes attract criminal liability apart from mere exclusion. The U.K. law also allows interviews to take place outside the station.

Nigeria's legal framework for protection of suspects' rights while obtaining their statement is not elaborate enough to reduce deliberate breaches to the minimal. Machineries are needed to implement the laws for effectiveness. Urgent reforms with the adoption of PACE, 1984, (as amended) and its Codes will reduce wrongful convictions and miscarriage of justice.

The chapters in this book give a lucid and in-depth analysis to legality of confessional statement in respect to rights of the suspects, the Nigerian Police Force and Nigerian Criminal Justice System.

Dairo Titilayo Abosede
LL. B, B.L, LL.M., Ph.D
aboseddairo2013@gmail.com

FOREWORD

This book titled "Extraction of Confessional Statements: The Suspects and the Criminal justice System in Nigeria' is a must have book for every stakeholder in the criminal justice process in Nigeria. It provides theoretical and practical concepts on effective administration of criminal justice system in Nigeria. The author examines relevant substantive and procedural laws on suspects' right in criminal proceedings from the time of arrest, interrogation at the police station to eventual arraignment in court. The book highlights areas of likely infringement on the rights of the suspects at the preliminary stages of criminal process and appraises the consequences of wrongful convictions that may ensue from inappropriate investigation by the Police.

The author dialectically evaluates the contending issues of promoting course of justice and according the suspect accused of criminal infractions fair trial. The book adopts comparative approach by drawing current pattern and trends in the United Kingdom on the rights of suspects under criminal justice system to postulate reforms in the Nigerian Criminal Architecture for the advancement of fair trial in the dispensation of justice by the Nigerian Courts. I am of strong conviction that this book will be useful to Judges, Magistrates, Lawyers, Police Officers, the Officers of correctional Homes and the general public as a modest contribution for the advancement of criminal justice in the overall interest of the Nigerian society.

Prof. Adeniyi Olatunbosun,
Former Dean,
Faculty of Law,
University of Ibadan.
Currently, The Vice Chancellor,
Kola Daisi University
Ibadan, Oyo State.

TABLE OF CASES

Adekunle vs. State, S/C 30th of June, 2006

Arogundade vs. The state (2009) 1FWLR, Part 481, 2099

Akinmoju vs. The state (2000) 6 NWLR (pt.662) 60

Abacha vs. Fawenhimi (2001) CHR 20 at 42

Agenu vs. State (1992) 7NWLR Pt. 256.749 C.A

Amachree vs. Nigerian Army (2003) 3 NWLR (PT.807) 256 272-280 C.A

Abubakar vs. The State (1969) NSCC 6

Arizona vs. Fulminate (1991) U.S. 279

Awolowo v. Usman Sarki Minister of Internal affairs (1960) 1ANLR

Babalola v.The State (2017) LPELR- 42365 (CA) 10

Bram vs. United States U.S 1897, 53; 542- 543

Brown vs. Stott (2001) 2 W.L.R.817

Brown vs. Mississippi (1936) 297 U.S 278

Chief J.E Oshevire vs. British Caledonian Airways Limited, (1990) 7 NWLR (Pt.163)

Chibuike vs. State (2011) 1 FWLR (Part 559) P. 1172 @ 1176

Condroun and Condroun vs. United Kingdom (2000) 31 EHRR 1

Connolly vs. H.M .Advocate (1958) S LT 79

Colorado vs. Connelly. U.S 1986

Danjuma vs. Kano State, 2018, C A, LPELR-44724 (CA)

Dawa vs. The State (1980) NSCC 334

Daniel Sugh vs. The State (1988) 5SCNJ 10

Escobedo vs. Illinois (1964) 378 U.S 478, 489

Emmanuel Olojede vs.The State (2018) LCN/10701(CA

Emeka vs. State (2010) 1WRN, 41

Egboghonome v. The state (1993) 7NWLR (PT.306) 383

Frazier vs. Cupp (1969) 394 U.S. 731

Haynes vs. Washington (1963) 373 US 503

Iorver & Ors vs. State (2013) LPELR 20783 (CA)

King vs. Warickshall (1783) K.B168 Eng. Rep. 234

Lamchi-Ming vs. R. (1991) 3 ALL ER 172 (@) 178

Leyara vs. Demno U.S 1954

Maeze vs. State (2004) All FWLR PT.202

Mbang v. State (2009) 18 NWLR (Pt. 1172) 140

Miranda vs. Arizona, (1966) U.S 384 @456

McKinney and Judge vs. R. 1991 98 ALR.577

Nwigboke & ors. vs.The Queen (1959) 4.F.S.C 101 p.102

Nwachukwu vs. State (2001) LPELR. 6183 C.A. Pp.22-23

Obidiozo & ors. Vs. State (1987) 4 NWLR (Pt. 67) 748, at 760 – 761.

Ogbu vs. The State (2000) FWLR (pt. 147) 1124-5, 11-27 C.A

Opper vs. U.S (1954) U.S, 348, 84, 89-90

Osuolale vs. The State (1991) 8 NWLR, Pt. 212, 770

Olmstead vs. United States (1928) 277, U.S 438, 485

Onochie v. The Republic (1966) NWLR 307

Osun v. State (2012) Vol. 6-7 Pt. II MJSC 1

Queen vs. IGP (1957) NNLA 25

R. vs. Thomas (2006) the Criminal Law Review 121-131

R. vs. Sat. Bhambra (1989) 88 CR APP 55

R vs. Priestly (1967) 51 Crim. APP. R.1

R vs. Davis 1990 Crim. Law Review. 860

Re Proux, Sub Norm R. vs. Bow Street Magistrates Court, (2001) 1All ER 57

Regina vs Alladice, (1998) 87 Crim. L.R. 608

R vs. Moss (2001) 1All ER.57

R v. Mathews (1990) Crim. L.R. 190 C.A

R v. Maguire (1989) 90 Cr. APP.R.15

R v. Marsh (1991) Crim.LR. 455

R. v. Willis (1960) 1W.L.R 55 at 58

R.v. Smith (1969) 2Q.B. 35

Salina vs. Texas (2013) 570 U.S, 178

State vs. Gwonto & ors. 1983 3iLaw/ S.C.69/1972

State v. White (1982) 319 N.W. 2d 213

State vs. Mati Audu (1971) N W LR 91; 92

State vs. Madukolu (1972) 2ECSLR (Pt.2) 623

State vs. Olasheu (2012) All FWLR (pt. 614) 152

State vs. Patton (1993) 133 N.J.389

Tehan vs.U.S. ex,reelSchott (1966) 382 U.S, 406,41

Torti vs. Ukpabi 1984 SC .p.19; LPLER- 3259 (SC) Paras. L.E

Uwaekweghinya vs. State, (2005) ALL FWLR (PT. 259) 1911 @ 1930

Udo vs. The State. 372 U.S 335

U.S. vs. Bickel U.S (1999) 440 U.S. 648,65

Yemisi Adeyanju (2008) NWLR. (PT.1092)

Yesufu vs. State (2001) 2SC 114 at 125

CONTENTS

Dedication.. *i*

Acknowledgements .... *ii*

Preface.. *iii*

Foreword.. *iv*

Table Of Cases .... *v*

Introduction.. *viii*

Confessional Statements In Criminal Justice System 12

Methods Of Obtaining Confessional Statement..20

Types Of Confession 27

The Concept Of Interrogation And Interviews..47

The Concept Of Privilege Against Self-Incrimination..65

Suspect's Rights In Criminal Justice System...85

Legal Frameworks Regulating Suspects' Rights During Extraction And Recording Of Confessions 101

The English Model Of Legal Framework Regulating Confessions 132

References.. 156

Index.. 164

INTRODUCTION

The police is the gateway to the criminal justice system. Its duties under the law includes crime control, promotion of harmony, security of life and property. The Constitution of the Federal republic of Nigeria 1999 established the Nigeria Police Force by virtue of Section 214(6), while Section 4 of the Police Act, Cap P.19 as amended lays down the general duties of the Police.[1]

Formerly, community police operates through indigenous means. Oghi[2] in his works studied what is now known as the South South Nigeria, such places like *Okrika*, *Kalabari* and Nembe groups the *Sekiapu* club, *Sekenei* and *Ekine* perform Police duties. The *Ekpe* society featured amongst the *Efiks*, women sometimes perform Police duties in some areas, in the Northern area, places like Bata and *Nbula* in *Yola*, *Mbamto* the virgin priestess was instrumental to detecting crime. We have *Ilaris* in Oyo, *Odi* in *Ijebu*, *Emefe* in Ife &Ijesha, *Inotu* in Ishan, and the *Enilake* Ordeal at Uzere in Delta state.

During the colonial period, it was no hidden fact that Police services were used for the defence of the government in power and as a weapon of political control.[3] The functions and powers of the police were however exercised during this period and later within various legal frameworks. Presently different methods and techniques are employed by the police during interrogation including

---

1 Rotimi K. 2001 *The police in a federal state: The Nigeria experience.* Ibadan College press ltd. 301; Section 214 (1) of the 1999 Constitution establishes the Nigeria Police Force; Section 214(6) conferred powers and duties on the members of the Nigeria Police Force.;
Section 4 of the Police ACT, Cap P.19 lays down the general duties of the Police.; Section 4, the Nigerian Police Establishment Act, 2020.

2 Oghi F.E. 2013, Reflections of Africa 's security situation: an examination of Nigeria Police Force (1999-2011) An *Africa Journal of Arts and Humanities,* Barhi Dar Ethiopia" Vol. 2
, No 4, 117-133.

3 Bittner E. 1975: *The functions of the police in modern society: A review of background factors, current practices and possible role models* New York: Jason Arinson ed. 14.

denial of food, isolation for a long time, cruel, inhuman and other degrading system. Famoye[4]noted that the consular guards began with 30 men in 1861 but was later renamed the Hausa constabulary in 1863 consisting of 600 men.

Originally a national and local police force existed simultaneously in Nigeria until dissolved by the military owing to complaints of bribery, bad training and standard, political partisanship and brutalization of opponents.[4]

Section 4 of the Police Act[5] empowered the police to prevent and detect crime, apprehend offenders, preserve law and order, protect life, property and proper enforcement of all laws and regulations. In the course of their law enforcement duties, an individual detained shall not be handcuffed or chained or unduly limited without a judicial order or as provided by law. Restraint is only allowed where there is violent reactions from suspects, to prevent escape and for safety of the suspect. By Section 37 of the Nigeria Police Force (Establishment) Act, 2020, Torture is prohibited while by section 5 of the Act. Legal services should be provided for an accused person where necessary.

Suspects and accused person bound with handcuffs, leg cuff or waist cuff of metal chain with lock is a terrible sight to behold and nothing can be regarded as more degrading or inhuman than to drag a human in chainslike a dog or binding two suspects without any weapon or show of any sign of violence or resistance. Also going by the Nigeria Police Code, of January 10, 2013 police officer use responsibly, the discretion invested in his position and exercise

---

4 Famoye A.D .2012. A historical survey of amalgamation of the Northern and Southern police departments of Nigeria in 1930. *European Scientific Journal vol.8* no 18:1857-788 (print) e-1857-7431

5 Section 4 of the Nigeria Police Force (Establishment) Act, 2020, reiterate the general duties of the Police. The Police while making arrest has a duty to inform suspect of his/her right to remain silent or avoid answering questions until after consultation with a legal practitioner of his choice. It is now mandatory by the new Act for the police to guarantee rights of suspects and ensure free legal

it within the law. The use of force is only permitted within reasonable measures in all circumstances and after discussion, negotiation and persuasion have been found to be inappropriate or ineffective; though unavoidable in some cases, police officers are expected to refrain from unnecessary infliction of pain or suffering and not make use of it. The use of firearms by the police is often abused to commit, cover up and justifies acts of torture and other ill-treatment.

By the Criminal Procedure (Statements to Police Officers) rules 1960 a police officer in the course of investigation can ask questions from anyone suspected or not, from whom he believes helpful information can be acquired but with caution given. It is after a reasonable suspicion that a complaint will be made to court.[6] Caution can still be administered after a statement is made if it was given earlier, where such individual is an illiterate, the statement may be read or interpreted to him by someone other than a police officer, maximum compliance with the Rules is expected from police Officers.

Where, however, non- compliance is discovered such as torture resulting in injury to the suspect who gave confessional statements while in the police custody where he was tortured; the same is not admissible and cannot support conviction. In such a case the public is at disadvantage as guilty suspects are thrown back on the society to perpetuate more crime. In *Maeze v. State*, with the evidence of torture resulting in injury to the leg of the suspects, the alleged confessional statements was not admissible in evidence to support a conviction.[7]

---

6 I have decided to make a complaint against you before a court do you wish to make a statement? You are not obliged to say anything unless you wish to do so, but whatever you say will be taken down in writing and may be given in evidence.

7 (2004) All FWLR Pt. 202.

1

CONFESSIONAL STATEMENTS IN CRIMINAL JUSTICE SYSTEM

The statements given by a suspect are important in the sense that they are used to establish a case or prove the commission or otherwise of a crime. Section 28 of the Evidence Act, 2011 defines a confessional statement as an admission made at any time by a person charged with a crime, stating or suggesting the inference that he committed that crime.[1] A suspect who makes a statement and admits to the crime, is said to have made a confessional statement. Creditworthiness was traditional while voluntariness rule makes inducements, threats and much later oppression as circumstances that vitiates confessional statement. This practice persisted in the common law courts of England until the seventeenth century and was widely used in France, Spain and other countries.

Confession history predates the twelfth century, but under the impact of the Roman law, which used torture to acquire confessions, it grew with extensive recognition. By the seventeenth century it gained grounds in the England's common law courts and was very prevalent in France, Spain and other jurisdictions. There was an indication in England by 1957 that the use of torture had become acceptable when Lord Coke, an advocate of the right to silence engage in the use of it.

Torture was later restricted and almost completely eliminated in order to prevent abuses by the police leading to unreliable confession. The English case of *King v. Warickshall*[2] excluded an

1 *Adamu vs. State* (2016) LPELR- 40326 (CA) p.22 Paras. E-F)

2. 168. Eng. rep. 234 (K.B.1783)

unreliable confession from evidence differentiating it from credible confessions. Thus a free and voluntary confession deserves the greatest credit because it is assumed to flow from the greatest sense of guilt and is therefore accepted as proof of the crime to which it relates; but a confession forced from the mind by the flattery of hope, or by torture or fear, is questionable if it should be admitted into evidence that no credit ought to be given to it and should be.

Confessions are the cornerstone of most criminal trials when written down, and it is still a major yardstick for police investigation.[3] There are also many decided cases holding that confession has the greatest position of authenticity when it is demonstrated beyond reasonable doubt.[4] It is judged in the annals of wrongful convictions as extremely and powerfully incriminating but with high susceptibility to error. It is also settled that like an admission in the civil procedure, confessional statement is stronger than the evidence of an eye witness.[5]

Section 28 (1) of the Evidence Act 2011 provides that confession is an admission by an accused person of a crime. It is a specie of admission which may be excluded on some grounds based on section 29(1) (2) (a) & (b) which provides that in any proceedings where the prosecution proposes to give in evidence a confession made by a defendant, it is represented to the court that the confession was or may have been obtained:

(a) By oppression of the person who made it or

(b) In consequence of anything said or done which was likely in the circumstance existing at the time, to render unreliable

3 Ibraheem, O. T. 2013 the Relevance of Confessions in Criminal Proceedings.

4 *Osun v. State* 2012 Vol. 6-7 Pt. II MJSC 1; *Mustapha Mohammed v. The State* (2007) 11 NWLR (Pt. 1045) 303

5 Basil vs. State (2008) 163 LRCN 186 at 192 Ratio 9

any confession which might be made by him in such consequence. In such circumstance, the court shall not allow the confession to be given in evidence against him

The courts through plethora of cases has made judicial pronouncement that a confession though made orally is strong as written extra judicial statement and sufficient to sustain a conviction.[6] Confessional statements are tendered at trial by prosecution as res, as something the investigating police officer obtained during his investigation and not as a proof of the truth of statement.[7] Oppression which includes torture, inhuman or degrading treatment , the use of threat of violence whether or not amounting to torture,[8] vitiating factors like coercion and undue influence if proven at trial is usually fatal to the prosecution's case where proven.[9]

Section 82, of the Police and Criminal Evidence Act, 1984 defines confession as include statement wholly or partly adverse to the person who made it, whether made to a person in authority or not and whether made in words or otherwise. Great emphasis is on the protective principle and the reliability principle as the foundation of PACE, the situation is the opposite in Nigeria. In *Arizona vs. Fulminate*,[10] a sharply divided U.S Supreme Court held that coerced confession need not be excluded from trial without proper evaluation like any other evidence with the trial judge deciding whether the error was harmless. Where examined and the confession shows harmful error thereby affecting the

---

6 *Agenu Vs State* (1992) 7NWLR Pt. 256.749 C. A; *Akinrinlola v State,* (2016) LPLER 40641 –(SC); *Danjuma v Kano State,* 2 018, C A, LPELR-44724 (C-A); *Taiye V. State* (2018) LPELR- 44466 (SC)

7 *R. v.Willis* (1960) 1W.L.R. 55 at 58;

10 *Arizona vs. Fulminate* (1991) U.S. 279; *Ojegele vs. State* (1988) NWLR Pt.71 414; Confessional statement not made freely and voluntarily cannot be admitted in evidence.

constitutional right of the defendant, it becomes more serious error than a simple technical one and the evidence must be excluded. The protective principle concerns the probative importance of evidence and, more usually, the fairness of the accused's trial.[11] Exclusion from a courts' proceeding of any evidence illegally obtained is symbolic in that if police violates suspects' right and there is no punishment it will be breeding contempt of law and thereby inviting anarchy. There is also the discretion of the judges[12] based on fairness to suspects, avoidance of breach of Judges Rule and administrative directives particularly the deliberate breaches which are not accidental. This is so as not to purchase the theoretical purity too dearly if we fail to acknowledge certain minimum standards for the treatment of suspects or having defined such standards to allow evidence acquired in breach of it to be used against an accused person.

Belgore JSC explaining the provision of the Evidence Act on confession introduced a new dimension to the definition of confession stating that an accused person's statement could be a confession or a denial and that confessional statement was only a phrase coined by the courts. In *Uwaekweghinya v State,*[13]the confessional statement was not clear but it described how the deceased attacked the accused and how he defended himself, the statement was adjudged not a confession but a clear explanation of what happened and thus an unqualified voluntary admission. Thus, until proven in court, a confessional statement though referred to as such, is not a substitute for sufficient, admissible and provable independent facts which would most probably guarantee a conviction and it could be subsequently retracted by

---

11. *Olmstead vs. United States (1928)* 277, U.S 438, 485 Justice Brandels dissenting, It is believed that in some parlance the exclusionary rule results in the release of the guilty , example is O.J Simpson whose release was based on the blunders of officials.

12 Section 78 PACE

13 (2005) ALL FWLR (PT. 259) 1911 @ 1930 S.C .29 @ 44

14 Section 31 of the Evidence Act

the accused or rejected by the court on some evidential or technical ground. A confession is not simply vitiated, because it was written as a result of a promise, of concealment or as a result of trickery practiced on an accused person while acquiring it, or produced in response to questions asked or having not been advised not to make the statement and proof could be provided.[14] In James *Igbiniova v. The State,*[15]the accused statement was made out of deception and admitted as proof for conviction, an indication that the doctrine of entrapment is not applicable to Nigeria as evidence obtained by means of deception is not rendered inadmissible by reason thereof. Obaseki JSC, advised that an improvement in the means of investigation and detection of the perpetrators to meet up with the increase in the rate of crime by all means allowed by our law.

Andrew,[16]looking at how the courts can protect the innocent from conviction and punishment opined that confessional evidence should not be admissible unless it is corroborated by other evidence. A confessional statement which is corroborated by any iota of evidence, no matter how small, is most likely to be an expression of truth from the accused person, if there is nothing to corroborate the facts outside the confessional statement, there is a probability that the confessional statement was acquired under duress.

In jurisdictions like America,[17]corroboration of confessional evidence that the offence in question has been actually committed is by proof of a *corpus delicti* of facts known by the perpetrator alone and not the one acquired from other sources. If there is nothing to corroborate the facts outside the confessional statement, there is a probability that the confessional statement was written

15 Igbiniova v. The State

16 Choo A.L.T.1991, Confessions and Corroboration: A comparative perspective *The Criminal law report law,* 867-876

17 *Opper v. U.S* (1954) U.S 348; 84,89-90

with coercion.[18] The fact that an accused person ran from the scene of crime and attempted to avoid detection by hiding the presence of a shot gun with two spent shells were held to be incriminating circumstances which connect defendant with the crime. In Nigeria, the law is no different in that confessional evidence must be corroborated to determine its veracity. The aim is not to determine whether the accused made the statement, this is determined by the judge in his fact finding capacity at the conclusion of the case, the focus at that stage is whether the statement is voluntary and therefore admissible.[19] In Scotland, there must be corroboration, additional evidence made available that tends to incriminate the accused. This is called special knowledge principle. In the circumstances surrounding the case of Connolly, it was held that[20]by section 77 of PACE, the jury is usually warned to be cautious if the contents of the confessional evidence is wholly or substantially uncorroborated and no corroboration of the making of a confession is available. This is also similar to the decision in *McKinney and Judge V. R.*[21]

This translates to the fact that the reliability of confessional evidence may be indicated by two types of corroboration. The first one requires a precondition to admissibility and corroboration of the contents of the confessional evidence while the other is about the making of the confession e.g. the atmosphere, isolation, powerlessness of the suspect in police custody and fabrication that makes signing a false document real. Corroboration by an independent material which unmistakably confirms the making of the confession or by audio visual recording, therefore lack of

18 *State v. White* (1982) 319 N.W. 2d 213 p.214

19 Ochem, C.M.2011,the Relevance of confessional statement in Criminal Proceedings in Nigeria, *Igbinedion University Journal of Jurisprudence & public Law* Vol.1, no. 2,2011p.2

20 *Connolly v. H.M. Advocate* 1958 S.l.T.79.

21 1991 98 ALR.577; 65 A.L.J.R.

recording facilities as we have in Nigeria today is disadvantageous to the suspect. If the jury is not satisfied, it leads to exclusion.

In *Yesufu V. State*[22]IguhJ.SC. held that retraction from a confessional statement does not *ipso facto* render it inadmissible in evidence. Resiling or retracting a confessional statement altogether does not stop the court from acting on it, since such u-turn does not necessarily made the confession inadmissible.[23] There is however a need to test the truth of the confessions before acting on it.[24]R *v. Kanu* approved R *v. Sykes* laying down the tests as follows:

i. Is there anything outside to show that it is true?

ii. Is it corroborated?

iii. Had the accused any opportunity to commit the crime?

iv. Is the confession possible or consistent with the facts of the case?

Not statutorily provided for though, the tests as laid down in the English case of Sykes[25] and approved by R *vs. Kanu* has been relied on in plethora of cases including facts apart from the confession to support that it is true, no matter how slight, whether the accused person committed the offence and the commission feasible? Whether it is compatible with other facts proffered in evidence.

Prosecution therefore has a lot to do before trial begins. To the learned JSC, the word obtained connotes a demand which cannot be voluntary as it dissipates the effects of caution administers by the police,[26] an indirect demand on the suspect to talk as the accused person cannot be expected to keep mute after caution.[27]

22 (2001) 2SC 114 at 125

23 *Alarape vs. State*

24 *R v.Kanu* (1952) 14 WACA 30

25 (1913) 8 CAR 233; *Onochie V. The Republic* 1966 NWLR 307

26 *The state vs. Mati Audu* (1971) NWLR 9. 1- 92 *Nakunde vs. Jos* N.A. (1960) NMLR 52 (58-59).

27 *Queen v. IGP* 1957 NNLR 3.

Further, when a person is under arrest in a criminal charge, the police should caution before recording the statement of the accused, if he makes any. The police has no authority to obtain a statement from him, having told him, he is not obliged, to say anything. The Judges Rules is instructive in this case because even though it is a rule of practice, it is designed to prevent police officers from getting a written statement of a suspect at all cost. Involuntariness of the confession must also first of all be shown in a criminal trial after which the surrounding circumstance will be examined.

The Judges rule is very prominent amongst the rules recognized in custodial interrogation basically as it has to do with ascertaining whether a crime has been committed, prescribe the caution to be administered to suspects before interrogation in terms of time and place, before questioning began and ended with the person present, regulates the taking of written statements from suspects after the caution is recorded in full and signed by the suspect. One must however not lose the fact that the Judges rules are not rules with force of law and cannot override a federal law or substantive law.

It is similar to the criminal procedure (Statement to Police Officer Rules 1963) operating in the Northern states of Nigeria with caution being the main feature. Caution right is however reduced in power by the provisions of section 31 of the Evidence Act. Tobi JCA (as he then was) expressed the view that where the caution is not properly administer, judges can reject the statement, he further observed that Section 31 is one section that I hate because it drains so much from the effect of section 28making it less influential.

2

METHODS OF OBTAINING CONFESSIONAL STATEMENTS

Confessional statement can be obtained by way of interrogation with the police adopting different methods or tactics within it. It was found that the conditions that could vitiate a confession evidence under section 29 of the Evidence Act[1] is very narrow and does not cover practices and abuse of psychological dimension amongst the police.[2] There is a lot of emphasis on oppression[3] or unreliability as the major factor vitiating admissibility of confessions in Nigeria meanwhile instances of torture and psychological methods being used by investigating police officers to obtain confessional statements is becoming more rampant. It is referred to in some jurisdictions as maximization and minimization. Minimization of moral,[4] legal and psychological consequences of confession, minimized with such words like you will feel better after confessing.[5]

1 given in consequence of anything said or done which was likely in the circumstances existing at the time to render unreliable any confession which might be made by him in such consequence "

2 Wald, M. 1967. Interrogations in New Haven: The impact of Miranda. Vol. 76 *Yale law Journal,* Iss 8,1519-1648; Gudjonsson, G.H. 2003 *The psychology of interrogations and confessions:* A Handbook. Wiley U.S.A. p. 27

3 Oppression was originally understood as being directed towards ensuring that the suspect was treated in a civilized manner by his interrogators.

4 that you are still a good person (moral minimization)

5 Inbau et al, 2001, Criminal *Interrogation and confessions,* 4th Edition Aspen publishers, 639

Third degree methods like physical violence, beating, kicking, or mauling suspects and torture is rampant, particularly with the Special Anti-Robbery Squad.[6] New methods of obtaining confessions from suspects are springing up every day which are worse than physical violence. The effects of this is large number of coerced false confession,[7] Factors affecting coercion including the use of baits, relentless and aggressive interrogations for over 6 hours and other factors or combination of factors. The Emotional questioning is characteristically compelling too and forced, to the extent that it relies on sustained force, manipulation and deception.[8] Some other identified tactics of interrogation used by the police includes:[9]

a. Sentiments based on personal reasons
b. Placing facts of guilt before the suspect
c. Weakening suspect's story
d. Interviews based on personality character
e. Telling suspect to cooperate
f. Giving decent / emotional reasons to justify the allegation
g. Placing false facts of guilt before suspect
h. Using compliments or sweet talk on the suspect
i. Reasoning with the suspects based on the qualification of the investigator
j. Reduction of the implications of the gravity of the offences

---

6 National Human Rights Commission overhaul of SARS and investigation of the human right abuses of victims of SARS, 3-man panel chaired by Justice Aguoma of Abia State High Court was set up on August 14, 2018 to investigate SARS and recommend redress for victims of SARS; Presidential Panel reform SARS. Southwest zone, sitting in Lagos from13th to 17th November.

7 Wickersham Commission Report, 1931. *The American Journal of Police Science* Vol. 2, No 4 (July Aug, 1931) pp.337- 346.

8 Current Law Enforcement Objectives and Practices in the U.S.

9 Leo. 1996a; Inside the interrogation room, *the Journal of Criminal law and Criminology*, 86,266-203

The use of any of the above named methods makes suspects to think that he or she actually commits the offence and his claim of innocence cannot get through, believes he has no choice as a result of which he becomes weary with no hope of getting out of an unbearable traumatic experience. The Police also sees suspects as detainees or accused person hence, emphasis on confrontational techniques instead of the police being equipped towards the productive and ethical ways.

In *R vs. Fulling,*[10] unreliable confession provided in Section 76(2)(b) of PACE was interpreted to include confessions obtained with inducement, promise of bail or that the suspect will not be prosecuted. It also includes aggressive interview, inaccurate record, absence of caution, unavailability of appropriate adult as required, non-compliance with the Codes of practice; lack of adequate rest before interview and lack of legal advice or ineffective representations by appropriate adult.

Others include non-compliance with procedures in relation to location, timing, duration and recordings of an interview are potential points for making the confession inadmissible in evidence. Where a confessional statement is objected to for having been taken under conditions stated in subsection (a) & (b) of Section 29, a trial within trial follows for the prosecution to prove that the confessional statement (not withstanding that it may be true) was not obtained in a manner contrary to the provisions of this section.[11] Challenging a confessional statement under section 78[12] of PACE does not usually involve a trial within trial except when

10. (1987) 2 AH ER. 6J; Definition of oppression approved in R v. Pager (1972); in*Rv. Prager,* lord MacDermont referred to it as questioning which by its nature, duration or other attendant circumstance so affects the mind of the suspect that he will crumble and speaks when otherwise he would have remain silent; Decision in *Rv.Prager* represents the common law definition of oppression.

11. *The State v. Usman Isah & 2Ors* (2012) 7SC (Pt.111) 93; *Emmanuel Eke v. The State* (2011) 1-2 SC (PT.1) 71; *Chuckwuka Ogudo v. The State* (2011) 1-2 SC 9Pt 11) 219

12. *R. vs. Fulling* (1987) 2 AHER.67

the defence challenges admissibility under both sections 76 (2) a & b and 78 of the law. By section 76 (4), confession itself may be excluded, based on facts discussed above or as a result of manner of speaking, writing or expression of the defendant. All these could be given in evidence.

Interrogations Method

In Nigeria, there is no statutory provision for the effective control of investigating police officers engaged in the abuses of rights of suspects during the extraction and recording of confessional statement save as the enforcement of the victims' fundamental human rights for wrongful arrest as provided by the 1999 constitution. In 2017, the Anti- Torture Act criminalized torture and provided that a victim of torture can file a complaint to the relevant Authorities. The ACJA, 2015 sees any abuse on the part of the police as a misconduct, in fact enforcing compliance with the provisions of the Act is vested in the Courts and other major stakeholders of the criminal justice.[13]The question is how many of such misconduct have or are being reported?

Under Police and Criminal Evidence Act 1984 PACE, there are provision designed in the law to control procedures, recognized any error or omission in any interview that can vitiate a statement This includes the requirements for the holding, handling and interview of suspects not related to terrorism in detention by police officers. Code E, 2016 is on audio recording of interviews, Code F is about visual recording with sounds of interview with recording of the suspect's voice not under arrest. As a result of this development, breaches are very minimal and it is not just about the exclusion of evidence but criminal liability is involved. It is also noteworthy that recording of confessional statements in the U.K have gone ahead of administration of caution only,

---

13 Section 2 (1) of the ACJA, 2015

combining it with the monitoring control. A criteria for its enforceability is failure to provide caution.

PACE Codes set out further rules to be followed by an investigative police officer and has a peculiarity of easier amendments than Acts of Parliament which is an advantage. The Code of Practice was reviewed in 2002, subsequently in 2004, 2006, 2011, 2017and 2019 and further supplemented by annexes and notes for guidance to aid interpretation. There are also models of interviews which were introduced; which an average Investigating Police Officer must follow such as PEACE which represents Preparation and Planning, Engage and Explain; Account, Clarify and Challenge with Closure and Evaluation.

Supervision of administration of rights of suspects at pre-trial stages is essential if abuses and violation of laws will be reduced. It was found that supervisors' major input is only in name on the statement of the accused person as a superior officer which is not sufficient.[14] Under the English law, the competence and integrity of officers that would supervise a lower rank officer involved in the investigation was found low, yet it was crucial to prevent the miscarriage of Justice. It was found that the ethos of individualistic approach and competitive results orientation amongst the police does not further the main goal of investigation. Detectives pay little attention to formal training particularly in terms of good practice and procedures but rather learn on the job from more experienced officers on the job thereby allowing perpetuation of bad practices. It was found that in 17 out of 60 cases, mistakes rather than violations or police inappropriateness was responsible for the ineffectiveness of the police.[15]

---

14 Hirst, J. 1993. Royal commission research papers, a policing perspective. Police Research Series. Paper 6; Supervision of Police investigations in serious criminal cases Baldwin, J and Maloney T. Study 4 Ed. Gloria Laycock. Home office. London.

15 Ibid.

16 Ibid.

The structure and culture within the police affects the conduct and supervision of criminal investigations. The investigative styles as well as the supervisory and regulatory mechanisms are prone to error and malpractice which must be controlled to avoid a miscarriage of Justice. An introduction of a unit for monitoring efficiency and probity is not out of place. Training materials at all levels is necessary for effective service.

Observing discussions with relevant key personnel shows that Police procedures at pretrial stages requires monitoring of interviews effective recording of interviews of suspects.[16] It was also found that here in Nigeria, heavy reliance is placed on information from the complainant other than the use of discreet investigation. Other observations shows that the police is dynamic with phenomenon of investigation based on culture and types of crime with drastic measures used in extreme cases during investigation while use of discretion[17] is commonplace. Also:

i. The putting in place of quality control mechanisms was not given priority.

ii. Trained supervisors with due integrity and skills are lacking.

iii. The required organizational and cultural change to make it work is lacking.

Interviews and interrogation /questioning methods

It was found that the overly obtrusive or aggressive techniques used by the police in earlier times is gradually given way to the ethical approaches. Interviews method however remains a more robust way of obtaining confessions than by accusations, threats and violence. Methods identified in this study includes the Reid technique of a two staged technique of the non-accusatorial stage

---

17. Discretion is common sense that will not bring your name or family into disrepute.

and a nine step custodial interrogation of separation, positive hostility, coercion, use of false facts amongst others. The peace model is also identified with less confrontational approach.

In the U.K, an interrogation is conducted only when the investigator is reasonably certain of the suspect's guilt as suspicion alone cannot ground conviction but upon reasonable grounds linking accused person to the crime. In Nigeria the law does not recognize interactions between an arresting officer and the suspects outside the police station meanwhile, it is not as if the suspects always keep mum throughout; questioning and interrogation are therefore not separated while interviews inside the police station is isolated from all that have gone before. Only formal Interviews are considered leaving out a situation whereby a delay in interview would lead to injustice.

Most of exchanges that takes place outside the police station between suspects and the police are undisclosed, not known or recorded,[18] it was discovered that out of the 641 detainees interviewed in a police station, 31.5 % were interviewed before arrest and 8.15 had been interviewed before custody, most statements made outside the station may not be repeated during tape recording at the station. Interrogation is a progression and not a single incident or one- time event occurring in a police station, it cannot be isolated from all that has gone before formal station interview. This situation not been in focus diminishes the rights of the accused persons as not all that happened may have been totally captured.

18 Hirst, J. 1993. Royal Commission Research Papers, A Policing Perspective. Police Research Series. Paper 6; *The questioning and interviewing of suspects outside the police station*, study no. 22, Stephen Moston and Geoffrey Stephenson, Ed. Gloria Laycock. Home office. London.

3

TYPES OF CONFESSION

Induced Confession

By the provision of Section 29 (2) (a) of the Evidence Act, 2011, evidence of confessional statement obtained by way of oppression of a suspect is not admissible in evidence, while oppression includes torture, inhuman or degrading treatment, and the threat or use of violence whether or not amounting to torture. In practice, there is hardly any criminal case prosecuted by the police without reliance on confessional statement in proving the charge. In most cases, it is common for objections to be raised on the grounds that the police obtained those statements by acts of oppression such as, shooting suspects at the foot, beating and hanging them from the ceiling for long period to extract information and confessions, flogging suspects with whips, beating them with batons and machetes, threatening them with death, piercing private organs of suspects with pins or inserting of sharp items into private organs, threatening with death, using cigarette lights to burn suspects, all in the bid to cause psychological and mental torture and by denying them food and water for days.[1] Confessions obtained in this manner presupposes that the accused had falsely been self-incriminated.[2] The implications of this is that there may be wrongful conviction of the defendant at trial.

1 Okeshola, F.B.2013. Human rights abuse by Nigerian police in four selected states and the federal Capital Territory, Abuja, *British Journal of Arts and Social sciences* 13.242-250,244.

2 Ibraheem, O.T, 2013, The relevance of confessions in criminal proceedings. *International Journal of Humanities and Social Science* 3.21: (Special issue- December) 291-300 at 291.

Police induced confession is being discovered on a daily basis from researches into police practices, case laws and psychology. 15-20% of all DNA exonerations are from false confessions.[3] The amount is still regarded as a tip of the iceberg in comparison with the fact that many of such confessions are objected to at trial and excluded.[4] Many results in guilty pleas or plea bargaining, some not subjected to the technology of DNA, others for whom evidence is not available, minor cases that do not call for attention in respect of the verdict of the judge and those from juvenile proceedings that contain privacy provisions. This statistics notwithstanding, confession statement still remain the gold standard for prove of criminal liability.

Kassin,[5] observed that innocent citizens are usually misjudged in situations in interviews, wrongly arrested and interrogated, their rights to silence ignored, encouraged and induced to make false narrative confessions, which forms subsequent basis for conviction. A good example is the Central Park jogger's case where innocent persons who confessed to an offence were sentenced at trial and later exculpated.[6] Access to police reports, recordings of interrogation and trial books may be difficult to access for knowing and establishing the truth of a confession, whether a suspect is innocent, the rate and the incidence of false imprisonment.

The sample is therefore incomplete with the above information, particularly in developing countries like Nigeria, as the means of

---

3. 2000; http://www.innocenceproject.org/; Garret, 2008 Scheck, Neufeld, & Dwyer

4 This result for Nigeria is not known through the procedure of trial within trial.

5 Kassin S. M. et al. 2009, police – induced confessions, Risk factors and recommendation factors, *Law and Human Behaviour* 2010- 13.

6 Drizin & Leo, 2004, The problem of False confessions in the post DNA World, *North Carolina Law, Review,* Vol.82, 891- 1007

7 Canada (CBC News, August 10, 2005), Norway (Gudjonsson, 2003), Finland (Santtila, Alkiora, Ekholm, & Niemi, 1999), Germany (Otto, 2006), Iceland (Sigurdsson & Gudjonsson, 2004), Ireland (Inglis, 2004), The Netherlands (Wagenaar,2002), Australia (Egan, 2006), New Zealand (Sherrer,2005), China (Kahn, 2005), and Japan (Onishi, 2007).

identifying vehemently opposed cases with false confessional statement and possibly induced confession is rather limited or unavailable. Proven false confessions are prominent in many jurisdictions but most case studys are based in the U.S and England.[7]

Estimating the extent of the problem in Iceland, personal reports methods were used on 509 inmates newly admitted to an Icelandic prisons over a 4 year period.[8] Another self-report studies of prison inmates in Iceland discovered that12% of 229 subjects (27), claimed they have made false confession to the police at one time or the other, a pattern regarded as part of a criminal lifestyle. In a more recent study amongst some inmates in the same place, false confessions was found to have increased.[9]Main motives for doing so being to protect someone (48%) and as a result of police pressure (52%) or so as to escape from custody. Similar studies were conducted using 138 student's experience samples with police interrogation in Iceland and Denmark. 78% of the suspects had never retracted their confession, 78% were convicted of the offences involved while college and older university students gave a self- report of false confession rated 3.7% to 7%.[10] 631 police detectives' respondents in a study conducted in North America gave an estimation from their own experiences of confession of 4.78% from suspects when interrogated even though they were innocent. This reports though subjected to cognitive bias and heavily motivated is however supportive of the fact that wrongful

7 Canada (CBC News, August 10, 2005), Norway (Gudjonsson, 2003), Finland (Santtila, Alkiora, Ekholm, & Niemi, 1999), Germany (Otto, 2006), Iceland (Sigurdsson & Gudjonsson, 2004), Ireland (Inglis, 2004), The Netherlands (Wagenaar,2002), Australia (Egan, 2006), New Zealand (Sherrer,2005), China (Kahn,

8 Sigurdsson et.al, 2001 False Confessions: The relative importance of psychological, criminological and substance abuse variables; *Psychology Crime and law* 7, 275- 289

9 Ibid

10. Gudjonsson, G.H. et al 2007 Custodial interrogation; what are the background factors associated with claims of false confession to police; *The Journal of Forensic psychiatry & psychology*, volume 18, issue 2. 266-275

11. False Confessions.org. Visited 18/11/17.

conviction exist but minimal in respect of innocent people forced into confession under interrogation. False confession may go relatively undetected in the courts and rarely retracted or disputed.

According to Innocence Project, false Confessions is third among the leading causes of wrongful conviction since 1980.[11] Other causes of wrongful conviction include false evidence from paid informants, insufficient or lack of defence, mishandling of forensic science, inefficiency on the part of investigators, false witness admissions and identification parade. In about six documented studies. 250 induced false confessions were found during interrogation, mostly with capital offences like homicides and other high profile felonies, while 80% of 125 false confessions occurred in homicide cases. [12]

Two thirds of DNA cleared homicide cases in the U.S.A were caused by false confessions with 30% of 317 post –conviction DNA exonerations are from outright confession or guilty plea. 18 of the 25% people exonerated through DNA had served time on death row, average age of exonerees at the time of their wrongful convictions is 27; 92% of which are men, 63% are under the age of 25, 32% are under the age of 18, 8 to 16% arrested for murder and rape are juveniles; 22% were mentally retarded and 10% had a diagnosed mental illness. In 2009, 22 new cases of DNA exonerated wrongful convicts with an overall number of 258, 351 DNA exonerations and 150 number of alternative perpetrators were also identified. Drizin and Leo studied 125 proved false confession, 70% were given by suggestible complied normally and mentally normal individual.[13]Roughly, 25% gave false confessions, virtually 68% officers in over hundreds of police jurisdictions believes that a suspect would confess falsely; 40% believe it is not very often, 28% believe almost never.[14]

12 https://www.innocenceproject (last visited 15/11/17)).

13 Drizin & Leo: 2004 The problem of false confessions in the Post DNA world, *NCL Rev.* 82 891-1007

14 Innocence project; Northwestern University School of law.

From the 1960s, police methods of interrogation has become entirely psychological in nature,[15] but in the U.S.A., there are still third degree methods like physical violence in form of thrashing, kicking and battering of suspects. Torture in form of dipping suspect's head in water, placing lighted cigars or pokers on a suspect's body and beating suspect with a rubber hose because it rarely leaves no scars.

Ofshe & Leo wrote that the modern equivalent to the rubber hose is the indirect threat, prolonged isolation without communicating with anyone, confinement, denials of sleep, food, and other needs. Others include extreme bodily discomfort, forcing a suspect to stand for hours on end, shining a bright, light on the suspect and obvious threats of bodily harm.[16]'These methods were in different forms and very common thereby resulting in large numbers of coerced false confession.[17] The third degree is given way gradually to psychological methods which is intrinsically compelling and coercive relying mostly on sustained pressure, manipulation, trickery, and deceit.[18] The result is that it tends to cause suspect to believe in being guilty, leaving him without a choice of no escape from the situation.

False Confession

False confession[19] are classified as Voluntary, Voluntary coerced,[20] Compliant and Coerced internalized confessions.[21] Ofshe & Leo[22]

---

15 Wald et.al 1967, Interrogations in new Haven: The impact of Miranda. Vol. 76 *Yale law Journal* 1519-1648 1967.

16 Richard Leo, 2009 *Police interrogation and American* Justice, Harvard University press, Cambridge Massachusset, and London, England. Chap. 230

17 Wickersham Commission Report, 1931 *The American Journal of Police Science* Vol. 2, No 4 (July Aug, 1931) pp.337- 346.

18 Current Law Enforcement Objectives and Practices in the U.S.

19 125 Proven false confession; 34% lasted 12 hours while 39% lasted 12 – 24 hours.

20 Blair,2005 any interrogation that exceed 6 hours is coercive

21 Kassin & Wrightsman 1985, Confession evidence, *The psychology of Evidence and Trial procedure,* S. Kassin and L. Wrightsman Eds.Beverly Hills Sage Publications, 1985. 67-94, 77

22 Ofshe & Leo 1997, Consequences of false confessions: Deprivations of liberty and miscarriages of Justice in the age of psychological interrogation, *The journal of criminal , Law & criminology, Vol. 88,No 2.436*

further divided false confession into, stress compliant; coerced compliant; coerced persuaded and non -coerced persuaded confession. Mccann modified it by adding coerced – reactive false.[23]

Voluntary False Confession

This is when innocent people admit being guilty of crimes they never commit without compulsion from the police and at other times even without any investigation or interrogation.[24] Reasons have been alluded to gaining undue public attention particularly for highly sensational cases within public glare.[25] Psychological reasons to inflict punishment on one self so as to assuage guilty feeling over prior wrongdoing, fantasy expressions, mental disorder and a desire to protect the actual perpetrator amongst other reasons.[26] An example is in 1947, when Black Dahlia, Elizabeth Short was murdered and over 50 women confessed to the murder, also in the 1980s, in Texas, Henry lee Lucas confessed to a number of unsolved murder cases, a situation considered as a very high-volume of confession ever.

Coerced Compliant False Confession

This is where innocent suspect confessed to a crime they know nothing about so as to be let off the hook, to avoid being punished, for a promise or implied reward. At other times to get a sleep, eat, to make contact to relations or friends, release, food or drug, to end the interrogation and prevent being held in custody.

---

23 Out of 205 wrongful convictions reviewed 18.40% were due to coercive confessions, none was due to false voluntary

24 Malelo F. A. and Campistol C., 2013, *Voluntary false confession as a source of wrongful conviction, the case of Spain; wrongful convictions and miscarriages of justices, causes and remedies in North America and European Criminal Justice*, Eds. Dans C.R. Killias M. Routdledge pp. 193-208.

25 In December 23, 2001, the then Attorney General for the Federation was assassinated in his house, and suspects said they were paid huge money by someone in Abuja, who they could not identify, (www.pulse.ng) news local Bola-Ige, visited 1/5/2018

26 At the kidnap of Charles Lindbergh's infant son, 200 people volunteered confession. 27*People of the state of New York v. Kharey Wise et.al* 2002.

Coerced compliant false confession leads to what is referred to as retraction during criminal trials like the 1989 Central Park Jogger's case where five juveniles confessed after a long-lasting questioning, they retracted their confessions but were later convicted at trial only to be set free three years later.

A 2013 study[27] provides new understanding of false confession by way of some investigations into the role of physiology and the effect of stress on suspects. It was found that suspects who are certain about their innocence, usually do not take police threats as very serious and they tend to put up resistance to police pressures, which can in the long run reduce suspect's resolve and lead to false confessions. Innocent suspects do take for granted the fact that they are innocent, become ill advised or even refused to take advice for invoking their rights to silence and counsel.

The state of innocence of a suspect actually determines the behavioral patterns of a suspect as a result of which misguided decisions are made which could be disadvantageous to them in the long run. The body languages of the innocent and the guilty are important for the purpose of determining how differently people with different state of mind construe things in the same situation. For example, the reactions of the innocent is synonymous with less stress, little or no state of apprehension, leading to failure to take appropriate steps where necessary.

Approximately 25% of accused persons who have been tried and found guilty and later exonerated had, in fact, confessed to the crime.[28] Under lab conditions, evidence reveals that one can begin to imagine and come up with a narrative that is totally false about the commission of crime[29] young adults may well also be led to

---

27 Guyll, M.et al. 2013, Innocence and Resisting Confession during Interrogation: Effects on Physiologic Activity, *Law and Human Behavior*. 37 366-375

28 The Innocence Project

29 Anon. 2015 study published in Psychological Science; The Economist.

generate richly detailed memories for committing crimes as their rate of recollecting memories for perpetrating crime was high as well as their rate of recollecting memories for non-criminal emotional issues and criminal issues are very similar. Additionally, ways by which false memories are recollected for crime also shared many characteristics with which true memories are recollected in normal situation.

The bluff interrogation technique used by an investigator, whereby they claim to have in their possession strong evidence that could be used against the accused person does not really affect an innocent person falsely accused but can frighten the guilty into confessing. A 2011 study[30] of a laboratory experiment testing the bluff technique relationship with confessions of the innocent parties shows 43 of 71 confessing to having pressed a computer key they were instructed not to touch, meanwhile they did not. Another 10% admitted to pressing the key to a study observer. A second group that tested respondent reactions to charges of cheating got an almost similar percentages of false confessions. It was observed that introduction of an innocent-affirming witness did not bluff participants from the accusations and pressures of the situation.

In another test group, 94% of participants were somewhat sure of their innocence, 24 (73%) were completely certain, 7 (21%) were somewhat to mostly certain, 2 (6%) said they were somewhat certain of their guilt. This certainty of innocence did not stop false confession as majority in the studies that agreed to consent, 75%, cited the bluff as the reason for that decision while others gave reasons as wanting to finish the study and feeling sorry for the experiment.

30 Perillo J.T. et al.2011, Conducted Inside Interrogation, The Lie, the Bluff and False Confessions, *Law and Human Behavior*, Volume 35, Issue 4, pp. 327-337. Subjects were instructed to complete a task, then were falsely accused of a transgression such as crashing the computer or collaborating with a colleague to improve their task performance. The experiment introduced variables such as bluff evidence, false evidence and less-than-honest eyewitnesses to identify which were the most likely to prompt a confession.

90% confessed, believing that a hidden camera had recorded their actions, while only 27% percent of control subjects did, others believe that their innocence may be, hence they waived their Miranda rights to silence and to attorney. However, they conclude that these experiments convincingly demonstrate that use of the bluff tactic in an interrogation can induce compliant false confessions from innocent people.[31]

Internalized False Confession

Suspects who are innocent but malleable have a tendency to believe whatever the police tells them of being involved in a crime they never committed even when they should not have.[32] The suspects' belief is seldom fully internalized, it is often called a persuaded false testimony, and some suspects do say that they are not sure of doing it, but they did it. At times they imagine they possess a split personality of being bad and good at the same time and acted out of a jealous attitude.[33]

Juveniles risk given an involuntary and false confession.[34] Gudjonsson[35] replicated an earlier study of 666 university students in Iceland, where 25%- 54% confessed. In another study into behavioral factors associated with confessions and denials with

---

31 ibid

32 Ofshe and Leo 1997, The consequences of false confessions: Deprivations of liberty and miscarriages of Justice in the age of psychological interrogation, *The journal of criminal , Law & criminology,* Vol. 88,No 2. Op.cit this footnotes with pp124)

33 Drizin and Colgan, 2004, Tales from the Juvenile confession front: A guide to how standard police interrogation tactics can produced coerced and false confessions from juvenile suspects; *Interrogations , confessions, and entrapment* G. D. Danniel Lassiter, Eds. U.20 New York, Kluvier Academic/ Plenum publishers.

34 Ibid

35 Sigurdsson & Gudjonsson, 1996a The psychological characteristics of false confessions: a study among Icelandic prisons; *Journal of Psychology, crime & Law* , vol. 10, issue 2

509 adult inmates and 108 juvenile offenders in Iceland, 62 (12 percent) of the adult admitted having made a false confession, none among the juveniles admitted such a confession. 35% proven false confession samples were younger than age 18 and 55% were aged 15 or younger.[36] All demonstrate the risk of combining young age with its attributes like vulnerability, dedicated obedience to authority, immature decision making abilities and psychological focused interrogation. It is suggested that psychological interrogation should therefore be avoided with Juveniles and suspects with low social maturity.[37]

Lay people also are ignorant of some interrogation tactics that are psychological powerful and can elicit false confession.[38] This is to the extent that after the plea is taken and a false confessor plead guilty and proceeded to trial, the Jury conviction rate changed from 73% to 81%.[39.] This confirms that it has been observed that confessional statements are innately and highly damaging to a defendant if not corroborated, proven or not.[40] Kassin observed that an electronically recorded confession should also be written down by the police as well as the suspect.[41]

False confession of innocent suspects may be difficult to be faulted because of the following:

1. Confirmation bias due to seeing confession as a behaviour countering self-interest but neglecting situational factors and

constraint.

---

36 Drizin and Leo 2004, The problem of false confessions in the post DNA world, *North East Carolina law Review, Vol. 82. 891-1007*

37 Inbau et. al. 2001.Criminal interrogation and confessions 639 Aspen Publishers, 4thEdition.

38 Leo and Liu, 2009 What do potential jurors know about police interrogation techniques and false confessions *Behavioural Sciences& the law* 27 (3) 381-99

39 Leo & Ofshe,1998 consequence of false confessions of liberty and miscarriages of justice in the age of psychology,*Journal of criminal law and criminology* vol.88, issue 2, 1-496

40 Kassin, S. M. 2006 A critical appraisal of modern police interrogation. *Investigative interviewing, rights, research regulation,* Tom Williamson, Ed.p. 207-228 Devon U.K.

41 Kassin et.al 1991 defines Maximization as "A hard sell technique in which the interrogator tries to scare and intimidate the suspect into confessing by making false claims about evidence and exaggerating the seriousness and the magnitude of the charges

2. Not all persons are good in detecting deception and there is an erroneous belief that whether lay people or professional, lies are separated from truth at high rates of accuracy, People cannot readily distinguish true and false confession as behavioral cues that are taught during the training of policemen e.g., gaze aversion, postural cues, grooming gesture are not synonymous with deception or lies. Content cues which are presumed to be associated with truthfulness are also present in confession such as, leading questions, photographs, visits to the crime scene and other second-hand sources invisible to the naive observer showing why the offence was committed.

3. Others include cues like revenge, jealousy, provocation, financial anxiety, peer pressures leading to mistake. These contents make it difficult to fault some confession as false.

Tactics of Extracting False Confession

This includes the use of situational and interrogational factors such as prolonged detention in custody, isolation, confrontation, presentations of false evidence and minimization which influences the voluntariness and reliability of confession.

Maximization and Minimization: These are necessary interrogation tactics used by trained interrogators with themes, scenarios and promises to induce suspects. The use of maximization[42] and minimization, false evidence ploy and other forms of techniques is linked with false confession.[43] Police detectives understand the importance of the post admission phase of interrogation as they use it to influence, shape and sometimes even script the suspect's narrative.

---

42 Out of 205 wrongful convictions reviewed 18.40% were due to coercive confessions, none was due to false voluntary

43 You are still a good person

Investigators persuasive skill coupled with the use of incentive towards extracting a confessional statement from a suspect eventually believing that he has a good reason for committing the offence characterizes minimization of guilt. By so doing, police officers, particularly Interrogators contributes the incidence of false confession by applying pressure on the suspect to believing a certain story and by being suggestive of facts of the crime.

Types of Minimization: The types of minimization are as follows:

1. Minimizing moral consequences
2. Minimizing psychological consequences of confession
3. Minimizing legal consequences of confessing.

Emerging Criminal Justice System data on the reasoning behind some interrogation techniques and confessions generally focused on understanding the causes of false confessions and how to reduce wrongful conviction. A 2013 project note report of scholars noted that wrongful conviction for murder cases occurs as a result of false charges and intentional wrong identifications, while for homicide cases it is as a result of high rate of official misconduct with74% of all false confessions in the database.[44]

Statistics have suggested that young people tends to admit guilt in a crime they did not commit. Thirty-eight percent of exonerations for crimes allegedly committed by persons under 18 in the last quarter century involved false confessions. This figure is comparably small with 11% rated for adults of 1,155 individuals wrongfully convicted and exonerated. Most countries are noted for prisons congestions, there is however new policies being put in place by Governments of such countries to specifically look into the issue of coerced confession particularly amongst young people.

44 Self defence e.g., provocation

It was discovered in a study that there are about 20 exonerations per year of defendants sentenced to death or very long prison terms in the United States.[45] Translated into relative proportions in Germany, it equals about seven exonerations each year for serving life or very long sentences. In France, five, one every second year in Switzerland. Conviction error is higher in the U.S than Europe, although it is not easy assessing the odds of innocent defendant being convicted.

In Europe, the police plays a far more active role in realistic terms since a confession obviously makes an acquittal far less likely, focus is not on the guilt or innocence of the accused person but on the sentence meted out by the court. There is no lie detection machine, no manipulative techniques of interviews including open ended questions, anxiety cues, and deception or presenting false evidence but certain violations do occur. In Europe, the police makes use of the information-gathering approach with the high probability of ending up with a true confession and thus reducing the likelihood of false confessions.[46]

The adversarial style whereby defendant is hard pressed to confess, with threats of harsher treatment in case of continued denial, leading to close ended question and alleged evidence that the police claim to have obtained in a 12 randomized trial was located and metanalysed.[47] Thong laboratory, based on field experiments, showed that confessions rate increased with the accusatorial

---

45 Sept. 8, 2013 report, National Registry of Exonerations statistics. The University of Michigan and Northwestern University law schools data compiled as part of the new National Registry of Exonerations.

46 Huff, C.R.2013. Errors occur everywhere but not at the same frequency. The role of procedural systems in wrongful convictions *Wrongful convictions and Miscarriages of justice; Causes and remedies in North American and European Criminal Justice.* Martin Killias, Eds. Routledge, New York and London Chapter 4; Cleen Foundation page 23 6/ 29/2005.

47 Redlich A.D and Meissner et.al. 2009 Techniques and controversies in the interrogation of suspects: The artful practice versus the scientific study Psychological Science in the courtroom: controversies and consensus:*Psychological science in the courtroom: controversies and consensus* Skeem et.al.Eds Guilford press (2009) 124-148

methods as well as the information gathering methods. Nigeria operates the accusatorial system; hence, the rate of wrongful conviction based on false information is presumably high like that of the United States.

Effects on the Suspects

A confession evidence is uniquely potent[48] in that it causes a neglect of facts in favor of the prosecution, overwrites any conflicting or exculpatory evidence thereby leading to the wrongful conviction of the innocent. In Nigeria, in spite of several warnings by the IGP to SARS against committing torture and the encouragement to follow due process,[49] torture is on the increase during the interrogation of suspect or detainees to extract information and confession.

Coerced confessions result in resentment and bitterness where there is an engagement of considerable proven evidence of coercion and manipulative interrogation techniques. It is the same story for innocent persons mistakenly arrested for suspicion and wrongly classified by detectives. The consequence is false confession, triggered off when police target an innocent suspect, and presumption of guilt starts. This leads to a contamination ofSuspect's post admission narrative leading to the elicitation and making of false confession.

Over 10 years compilation of report exposes the established use of police torture chamber with suspects not having access to lawyers, families and courts. Use of torture is common place and often used to extract confession with confession been used as a shortened way to quick conviction by the police. False confession results in wrongful conviction.[49]

---

48 Ibid

49 Http.//www.amnesty.ng/en/countries/africa/nigeria/right-riteria, visited 18/11/17. 2009/ reports of Amnesty international

The vulnerable, developmentally disabled, cognitively impaired, Juveniles and mentally ill suspects have limited emotional and social intelligence to understand communications or situations that are confrontational like police interrogations. They ought not to be handled in a certain manner to start with. They also suffer the effect of false information. Post admission narration and the contamination error makes narrating confession to become more than I did it, Suspects moved from denial to I did it and why I did it. Examples of such is Anthony Ray exonerated after spending 30 years on Alabama's death row;[50] Eric Kelly and Ralph lee Kelly after 24 years of wrongful conviction;[51] Kansas Mouri led the charge for son's exoneration after 23 years;[52] Supreme Howards overcame after 20 years; the Birmingham six were convicted for a life sentence in 1975 in the U.K for Pub bombings they were later exonerated on 14/3/1991. They later got compensation in tunes of millions.

Torture incidences were explained by suspects' relation in Nigeria to include beating of the suspect, to the extent of sustaining wounds on the back and body the police having used stick to hold the suspect between arms and legs after suspending him. According to the suspect's mother if she had not paid the officers involved, he would have been killed being the only child. The boy was released to the mother after the payment was made without any document like[53] bail bond. In 2007, UN special rapporteur found that that torture and ill-treatment are widely practiced in police custody and are intrinsic part of police practices in Nigeria.

In 2006, Human Right Watch gave reports of a boy of 16-year-old arrested by men of SARS in Anambra State who was threatened

50 https://www.innocenceproject (last visited 15/11/17)).

51 https://www.innocenceproject (last visited 15/11/17)).

52 Hinton was convicted of the 1985 murders of two fast food restaurant owners based upon the testimony of a state forensic examiner that the bullets in the two murders came from a gun found in Hinton 's house

53 https://twiter.com/innocence. 18/11/17.

to be killed except his father brought a sum of N100,000.00. He was beaten, with wounds on his back, suspended on his bed and was only released when his father paid.

Likewise in 2007, In Anambra State, a market woman told Human Right Watch that she was tortured with a tube tied around her arms from hands to shoulder for 6 hours before it was loosened. She was also caned on the arms while made to carry two blocks on the back for about two and a half hours.[54] For the Apo '6' of June 7th and 8, 2005, no one has yet been held accountable.

Cases of torture are rampant in spite of several warnings by the IGP to SARS against committing torture and encouragement to follow due process.[55] It was observed that caution warnings forms vary in words and communications, in 32% cases the forms filled shows that legal counsel could be obtained without charges. The knowledge and intelligence of waiver of rights by most suspect who is informed of their rights to caution is not very clear. Suspects that are with mental disabilities, adolescents below age 16 and 55% of 430 youths have impaired understanding of Miranda warnings as they often think they can't talk until they are told to. Also, when they are faced with decision making, they ask whether they can disobey authorities and they believe they should waive their right. Significantly the effect of Miranda on suspects are linked to low intelligence, desire to comply and belief that an innocent person cannot be unjustly punished.

Coerced confession causes erroneous conviction as the rate increases despite knowledge that there is element of coercion even by mock juries and being instructed to disregard the confession as inadmissible which shouldn't influence their verdict.[56] It biases evaluation by Judges, Leo observed that 73% of all confessions were erroneously convicted,[57] while 81% of 125 are false confessions.[58]

---

54 Father of 16-year-old boy arrested in Onitsha, Anambra State, April 19, 2009.

55 2009 reports of Amnesty international

56 Kassin & Sukel, 1997. Coerced Confessions and the jury, *Law Hum Behav.* 21-27-46

Confessions especially detailed ones in some cases are fatal to a defendant's case because judges in some jurisdictions finds it unacceptable that someone would confess to any crime in the first place. Consequently suspects who were tricked, deceived and coerced by the police goes through the trauma of disputing a lot during trial.

Coercion at pretrial stages also results in post trauma stress disorder which could last for years unless treated. Other effect include likelihood of suspects who gave confession being charged more than other suspects there is 25% likelihood of getting plea bargain and 26% likelihood of being convicted.[59]

Effects on the Criminal Justice System

Injustice at any segment of the society translates to threats to justice everywhere. Successes recorded in exonerations of the wrongly convicted through DNA testing across jurisdictions has announced the dawn of a new era and reform to the criminal justice system thereby reducing and preventing incidences of future injustice. With the advent of such exonerations by way of technology, the era of undermining the most basic of rights of a suspect by way of all forms of abuse by the law enforcement agencies at pre- trial stages is at end.[60]

57 Leo & Ofshe, 2001.The truth about false confessions and advocacy scholarship; *Crim. law Bull* 37: 293-370

58 Leo, et al.2006 bringing reliability back, false confessions and legal safeguards in the 21st century, *Winconson law Review* paper no. 2009-04,1-63

59 Gudjohnsson, G.H. 1991 Custodial interogations Why do suspects confess and how does it relate to their crimes, attitudes and personality. *American Psychological Association.* 12 (3) 295-306

60 Ehighalu, 2012 Nigeria Issues on Wrongful Convictions *University of Cincinnati law review.* Vol. 801136. Review 1136

Average number of cases a judge completes today within a twelve month period is between nine and twelve cases and[61] for criminal cases, it is rather low.[62] It is observed that the reason why this is so for criminal cases is due to shoddy investigation of cases by the Police. The police rarely investigate cases as expected but merely take statements from citizens on the basis of mere petitions, with no modern tools of investigation. How voluntary the statement of an accused person is determines the outcome of his case during trial. American courts treat confession evidence with mixed feeling of esteem and suspicion and once introduced, other phases of the trial becomes surplus supporting the fact that actual trial occurs when confession is obtained.[63]

Law enforcement officers, knowing so, have abused their power in this regard. History has also shown that confessions have often been extorted in some cases to avoid the trouble of conducting discreet investigation and information gathering.[64] A reliance which in the long run is disadvantageous as it makes the confession less dependable and prone to manipulations.[65] If the circumstances surrounding the taking of a confession is coerced, there is a risk of the evidence being ruled inadmissible at trial in spite of the truthfulness of the confession.[66]

61 Worrey F.A. 1983. *The prosecutor in public prosecutions* New /Ed.2000, Lagos State Ministry of Justice Law Review series. Arthur Worrey completed 31 cases before late Justice Rosaline Omothoso

62 A judge of the High court and a participant at the Network of Justice Sector Reforms (JRTs) Conference held in Cross River State on the 8th- 10th of May 2018 admitted that after finishing with like four records for civil claim, he is yet to go halfway with criminal record book.

63 A judge of the High court and a participant at the Network of Justice Sector Reforms (JRTs) Conference held in Cross River State on the 8th- 10th of May 2018 admitted that after finishing with like four records for civil claim, he is yet to go halfway with criminal record book.

64 *Colorado us Connelly*, 1986,

65 *Haynes v. Washington* 373 US,503,373, US 519

66 *Escobedo v. Illinios* (1964) 378 U.S 478,489

72 Ibid.

False confession leads to retraction of the confession or objection to admissibility, leading to a mini trial so as to prove the veracity of the confession. This often causes delay in the trial and congestion of the prison. It is still the leading and the most prejudicial source of false evidence that leads to wrongful convictions.

Overly dependence on confession as a centerpiece of the prosecution's case against a defendant creates lack of trust in the criminal justice system by the populace and particularly in the police; it undermines public confidence.[67] It further encourages police corruption, miscarriage of Justice as a result of coerced confessions which have undermined the public faith in the police and the judiciary as a whole.

It makes judges to be careful of the police and confession evidence to the extent of increasing acquittal rate. There is also the boomerang effect in that coercion of suspects can have a negative effect as a suspects may refuse to confess at all if the interrogation techniques is in the extreme. Retraction during trials are also rampant having made the confession under duress of giving information.

Confession in its evidential nature is like a bombshell that can shatter the defence of an accused person, presumptuously it is also believe that a defendant without a good defence lawyer and who has confessed is guilty and should be convicted. This is because claims of innocence by suspects or police misconduct are rarely believed while judges rarely throws out confessions except in some cases, even highly questionable ones. Confessional evidence are treated at trial with certainty of the guilt of the suspect and accused persons than circumstantial evidence except where backed up by a video or audio tape of the suspect committing the crime.

67 Ibid.

This is virtually true about all cases where the confession receives pretrial and trial publicity.

False confession data is still not available from both government as well as private organizations. This has made it equally difficult for researchers to study the pattern of its occurrence while great reliance has been on primary sources of cases from police reports, pretrial and trial transcript, and electronic recordings of interrogation to evaluate the unreliability of confession. Information about false confession not admitted into evidence, disproved at Mini trials, those that result in guilty pleas, those not subject to post conviction review[68] and those given to confidentiality are not accessible, even if available.

Real trial have been said to occur when confession is obtained.[74] Cases exonerated by DNA has provided for a window of some sort to the fact that wrongful conviction exists and given solution to a small part of a much larger problem in criminal procedure. DNA evidence is however not available in some cases while most rules in police manuals are based on experience rather than objective and scientific data, no one knows the rate of true or false confession as a result of which there is misrepresentation of facts.

---

68 Leo. R. 2009, False confession, causes, consequences and implications. *The journal of the American Academy and the law* 37,322-43

4

THE CONCEPT OF INTERROGATION AND INTERVIEWS

Interrogation is a higher level of questioning of suspect, it takes place on reasonable suspicion and after arrest for an offense to be investigated. Interviewing and questioning are the various stages of interrogation, terms referring to distinct phases of collecting verbal and written answers from a suspect; each phase varies on how the process of collecting data can and should take place. Police regard interrogation as mainly directed at obtaining a confession of guilt by questioning rather than openly investigating the reality of the participation of the suspects in the supposed crime.[1]In his remarks, Baldwin noted that police interrogation concerns future rather than previous occurrences and was used to acquire proof for use in court rather than to establish the suspect's real participation in the alleged crime. In *Emmanuel Olojede vs. The State,*[2] it was held that an accused can be convicted on his confessional statement alone where same is direct, positive and proved. There is therefore a high likelihood that a false confession will emerge from the interaction of the police with suspect. A domineering police officer who is very sure of the guilt of a suspect can pose a significant threat to a suspect in respect of the reliability of confessional statement, as the suspect may eventually succumb under such heavy burden.

---

1 McConville M. et.al 1991 *Case for the prosecution: Police suspects and the construction of criminality* Routledge Revivals. London. chapter 4 pp.56-79

2 2019 LCN/13161(CA)

It has come to be recognized that some psychological stress is essential to convince some suspects to confess when they are actually guilty. Remorseful criminals blame the offence on internal variables as a loss of momentary control, confessing to relieve their inner tension but are embarrassed to do so and therefore need some pressure to confess. However, the pressure could be excessive and transform into oppression. Until the 1930s,[3]the police's techniques engaged some type of coercion, such as threats, physical violent, torture heavy-handed and often deceptive tactics. In 1931, third-degree methods became rampant in the United States as police methods of interrogation and subsequently criminal defendants were sometimes wrongly convicted and jailed. Aggressive technique such as exposure to bright lights, cold water, and physical blows to obtain confession were also used.[4]In contemporary times, methods of interrogation is more psychological with the use of interviews and questions that are more objective, measured, and ethical. The objective is to discover the truth and not just to get a confession to a crime.[5]

With the use of these techniques, false confessions and incorrect judgment is the result as some innocent suspects do admit to the commission of offences they never committed under interrogation. By the 19th century, techniques of extreme interrogation like assurance of gaining freedom, profit or treatment would vitiate confession. The dangers of over dependence on confession was found in *Escobedo v. Illinois,*[6] where inducement led to the suppression of a confession because a teenager was induced to speak the truth no matter what having been charged for

4 Roberts k.2012 Police Interviewing of Criminal Suspects: A historical Perspective www.*internet journal of Criminology, issn2045-67431-17.*

5. Gehl R. 2017 Introduction to Criminal Investigation: Processes, Practices and Thinking http:/ www.w3.org/2000/svg Last visited 11/4/2018

6. 1964 (378) U.S ,478, 489

7. *Regina v. Garner* (1848), 169 Eng. Rep. 267, 267-68.

8 ibid

murder.[7]Under common law it was acknowledged that some confessions might be unreliable, leading to innocent individuals getting convicted.

The Van Meters approach is an ethical framework of interrogation and obtaining evidence from suspects by way of less hostile techniques.[8] The challenges of interrogation can be complex with the daily number of cases to attend to and the process can be compromised. The availability and the use of the right processes is therefore of essence to the outcome of the confession in court.

The Reid Technique[9] is an alternative of two-staged process of an inquisitional interview of suspect about certainty and trickery. The 1st stage of the interrogation has nine steps under custody of determination of the guilt of the suspect so as to separate suspects from informers or witnesses In the second stage, methods like isolation, optimistic confrontation, the interruption of denials and the presentation of false evidence, minimization, and various tactics for converting admissions into written narrative statements are used. It is noted that in Nigeria this is very common and the stronger the facts the more it is to believe the guilt of a suspect.

In *U.S. v. Bickel* [10]confession was extracted by five agents after high handed methods were used on the defendant who was acquitted later. The reason behind such an action according to one of the investigators is that the suspect showed 'signs of deception' and a body language in the sense that the suspect tried to remain calm but was observed as being nervous, eyes roaming

7 *Regina v. Garner* (1848), 169 Eng. Rep. 267, 267-68.

8 ibid

9 Inbau et al. 2001 *Criminal Interrogation and confessions*4thEdition Aspen publishers 639;

a vast number of law enforcement professionals in North America have been trained. 10 *U.S. v. Bickel* (1990) 30 M.J 277

11 (http://www.courttv.com/trials/tuite/). En. Wikipaedia.org/wiki/murd last visited on 22/9/18

at every question asked him, failure to make a direct eye contact, actions erratic and very emotional.

In Florida, Tom Sawyer was accused for the offence of sexual assault and murder after long hours of hostile interrogations of 16 hours, a confession was extracted with issued threats.14-year-old Michael Crowe and his friend Joshua Tread way were intimidated at a long and false interrogations into confession in a case of murder.[11]Sullen Michael Crowe was interrogated without counsel and discussion with his parents to avoid tougher investigation. In *Tunde Balogun vs. Federal Republic of Nigeria,*[12] the statutory provision as to recording of confessional statement was ruled on in regards to Section 17 of the Administration of Criminal Justice Act, 2015. It was decided in that case that failure of the prosecution to comply with the said provision in the recording of an accused person's extra judicial statement, will render such statement impotent and capable of being relied upon by the court to sustain a conviction.

Psychological questioning is emotional in nature with its consequences. In *R.vs. Thomas,*[13] an Australian citizen, Joseph Thomas, was arrested and imprisoned in Pakistan on suspicion of connections with terrorist organizations where he was interrogated by officials from the USA, Pakistan and Australia. On returning to Australia, he was alleged of terrorist –related offences, tried and convicted based on the self- incriminating statements made by him during his questioning by members of the Australian Federal police. It was held that Self-incriminating statements made by him in Pakistan when he was interrogated with caution as to his right by Australian Federal Police (AFP) should not have been admitted. His conviction was overturned, on appeal to the Supreme Court of Victoria, it was revealed that while Thomas was being interrogated in Pakistan, he was shown a photograph of himself

11 (http://www.courttv.com/trials/tuite/). En. Wikipaedia.org/wiki/murd last visited on 22/9/18

12 (2018) LCN/10701(CA)

13 (2006) V.S.C.A 165

with his wife and child, and a letter from his family and told to read the letter again at a later stage. After much questioning, he admitted that he had received money from Khaled bin Attash, an associate of Osama bin laden and that he had trained at the Al Farouq Camp. The confession was excluded because of denial to legal representation, inducements as he was asked to continue to cooperate with the interrogators; the statement was held under the Australian law as not voluntary. The Court is of the view that the Pakistani and Australian officials were persons in authority who can affect the course of interrogation and prosecution.[14]

Police researchers use interview-based decisions of reality and deception to obtain confessional statements thereby branding suspects that exhibit certain characteristics and treating them alike.[15]The effectiveness and the performance of this is however influenced by training and experience. Behavioral analysis and nonverbal cues of various measures including eye contact, hard face, sagging, attitudes of anxiety, disinterestedness, over guardedness as indications of deception. Some Reid associates investigators have been trained in using these methods to establish the truth at 85% accuracy rate.[16]

Some methods and techniques of interrogation apart from the Reid techniques include others like the guilt-presumptive, third degree, torture, extreme torture of terrorists and kidnappers suspects' other psychological methods, File and Dosier technique, We know all technique, Futility technique , Rapid fire technique , Matt Jeff or friend/ foe technique, Incentive technique(for stick and carrot) technique, Repetitive technique ,Pride and Ego technique, Silent technique and Change of scene technique. Four

14 ibid
15 Inbau, et al. 2001 *Criminal interrogation and confessions*4thEd. Aspen Publishers .639
16 ibid

stages of conducting interrogation were identified as the rapport building stage, information exchange stage, challenging stage and ending.[17]

Discretion by the police and coercive nature of most interrogations contributes an increase in studies into what is happening behind closed doors of an interrogation room.[18]In *Miranda vs. Arizona* the Court remarked that privately conducted interrogation results is so much covered leaving a gap in the understanding of what actually happens in the interrogation rooms. In Nigeria, information about tactics employed by investigating police officers for interrogations is highly secretive and not uniformly guided save as are found in various Police Manual and textbook.[19]

On the issue of whether this admittedly strong strategy could also make innocent people confess, Inbau et al.[20]is of the view that it is only used on presumed guilty at interviews preceding interrogation identified by either verbal or non- verbal body languages. The guilty and the innocent are then reliably distinguished while interrogation proceed accordingly.

It has been argued that trainings, rehearsals, or the highest of performance amongst police officers may not detect an accurate truth and judgment, [21] because with the trainings little successes have been reported and errors do occur.[22] As a matter of fact trainings at the Reid seminars have involved over 65,000 law

17 Momodu, B. 2013 *Law,Rules and Procedures of Criminal investigation in Nigeria*Evergreen overseas publications limited. 101

18 Leo, R. A. 1996a. Inside the interrogation room. *The Journal of Criminal Law and Criminology*,86, 266–303.

19 Zulawski, D. E. &Wicklander, D. E. 1993. Practical aspects of interview and interrogation. Oxford:

20 Ibid. It is advised that by analyzing an individual's verbal and nonverbal behavior during this initial questioning, interrogators can reliably distinguish between denials made by those who are guilty and those who are innocent and then proceed accordingly. To assist the police in making these judgments, specific training is offered on the analysis of verbal and nonverbal cues to deception.

21 Vrij, A. 1994. The impact of information and setting on detection of deception bypolice detectives. *Journal of Nonverbal Behavior*, 18, 117-136.

22 Mark A. et.al, 1990 Training Observers to Detect Deception: Effects of Self-Monitoring and Rehearsal. *Human communication research* vol. 16, issue 4, 603-604

enforcement experts attending the 3-day seminars over the previous 25 years.

In a study,[23] it was revealed that lying suspects may not be easily distinguished from those telling the truth as the signs are similar, some noticeable signs include anxiety, being hostile, fearfulness, inconsistencies in facts as observed by Simon[24] are some of this characteristics.

A number of reasons for ineffective questioning have been proposed. For example, lack of time, lack of staff in main custody interviews; inefficient staff undefined supervisory role of the police officers and the impartiality of the inspector.[25]Other variables include disputes between operational requirements and organizational goals, pressures and priorities, lack of training and supervisory capacity.[26]

Despite endorsing surveillance in principle, there are a number of variables that hinders its translation into practice. Such as lack of time, heavy administrative workload, job description not related, inefficient policy and compliance, opportunity costs too high in relation to potential benefits,[27]costs of routine monitoring impractical given current resources, under staffing, lack of written or recording materials and equipment for tape recording.[28]

Techniques of Interrogation Generally

Self-incriminating statements were prevalent within the Western Police in the 1990s[29] psychological interrogation making use of techniques like maximization and minimization, false evidence play

23 Fahey W. E. et al. 1987. False suspicion and the misperception of deceit. *British Journal of Social Psychology* 26, 41-46.

24 Simon, D. 1991. *Homicide: A year on the killing streets.* New York: Ivy Books.219

25 PACE

26 The presence of a supervisor could be seen as oppressive, supervision of interviews was not generally seen as part of the first-line supervisor's role, because officers were regarded as 'trained

27 The Metropolitan police

28 The Nigeria Police and the Metropolitan police in the U.K

29 Baldwin, J.1992 Videotaping police interviews with suspects- an evaluation. Police Research paper 10 London Home office

and other forms of deception are common amongst the police and have been frequently linked to false confession.[30]

Maximization: This is a collection of different of tactics targeted towards getting the suspect to belief that he or she is guilty and he needs not deny any of the facts. It includes making accusation, not allowing objections, suggesting facts to divert the suspect's strength and focus from self-confidence to bleakness. Means of inducement include the use of subtle warnings of harsher consequences in response to the suspect's denials[31].

Minimization: Minimization tactics are often employed by the police for interrogation. It includes minimizing moral, psychological and legal consequences. The first two is mostly used. With minimization, the interrogator offers understanding, normalizes and minimizes the crime. A police officer could offer, using himself as an example that he or she would not have behaved otherwise, he could also offer an alternative to suspect to make it look like the offence was spontaneous, a consequence of peer pressure provocation, accidental and not the work of another person. Leniency in punishment is offered if suspect confesses.[32]Themes, inducements, and talks of leniency are commonplace here.

Inbau observed that some promises given to a suspect by a police officer at pretrial stages can render a confession involuntary while others are not depending upon the circumstances.[33] For example, before the decision in the case of Miranda, deception can induce

---

30 Ibid.

31 Leo & Ofshe, 2001 The truth about false confessions and advocacy scholarship ,vol. 37, *Criminal law Bulletin 78 pages; Sage journals*

32 *Bram v. United States* 1897, U.S. A. 532 ; 542- 543 Bram's conviction was reversed based on the fact that t a confession must not be obtained by any coercion by way of any sort of threats or violence, direct or implied compromises, however slight.

33 Fred Inbau et.al 1997 *Criminal interrogations and confessions*, 5thEd. October 3, 2011, 1997,201

involuntary confessions but will not automatically invalidate the confession.[34]The use of trickery and deception as found in standard interrogation manuals contributed to the use of duress in a forced environment while obtaining statements. Miranda did not prohibit the use of these methods but gave some relief from the coercive effect of the use of some tactics and empowering suspects with rights which could frustrate the use of statements obtained from forced interrogation.[35] Deception by itself is not sufficient to render a confession involuntary, being one out of many others include false allegation, false reports, tapes and other evidence, stage managed audio tape of an alleged eyewitness account.[36] Others include promises of less punishment, lower prison sentence, prosecutorial or judicial leniency upon confession and vice versa, homicide framed as unintentional with self defence as an option.

Others includes false evidence/information obtained through other police witnesses, forged result from test conducted, fake norms and false physical feedback which can result in impaired and graphic judgments.[37] Offering suspects bail in return for confessions, threatening to charge close relation should they refuse to confess, holding them incommunicado for some time in a coercive atmosphere during interrogation are methods capable of causing suspect to confess involuntarily.[38]Trickery, cajole and persuasion,[39]denying a suspect of his right of silence are all methods of interrogation. Subtler forms of intimidation could also include the cane swinging policemen in the backroom when a nine year old suspect is being questioned; showing an offender a photograph of his father and remarking on its likeness to the accused in a way to gain his confidence. These are examples that

34 *Leyara Vs Demno* 1954; *Spano Vs New York*,1959, 9.

35 *Frazier vs. Cupp* US 1969

36 *State v. Patton*,1993.

37 In 1989, 17-year-old Marty Tankleff was accused of murder. On a presentation of false evidence, he became disoriented, confessed and was convicted on his confession which was vacated 19 years later.

38 Warren C.J Irving and Hilgendorf, Research study no:1 Royal Commission on criminal procedure

39 *Miranda, (1966)* 384, U.S @ p.456.

are familiar with experiences obtainable in Nigeria. There is also questioning without rest, interrogators pretending to have evidence of the suspects' guilt and excusing a behavior in order to downplay the moral seriousness of the act. The exercise of authority or power in an oppressive, punitive or wrongful manner, unjust or cruel treatment of suspects were further explained in *Amachree vs. Nigeria Army.*[40] The clamping of chains around the defendant's legs during interrogation and the making of confession amounts to oppression, rendering inadmissible the confessional statement. It is described in other parlance as the imposition of unreasonable or unjust burdens.[41]

Interviews Generally

Interviews has been given many descriptions in many discourse. Dennison[42]described an interview as any series of police-led questions for the purpose of an admission based on which trial can commence. It has also been defined as any debate or conversation between suspect and police officer.[43]It was later qualified that questioning an arrestee not far from when an offence was committed in order to elicit an innocent explanation did not constitute an interview,[44]as well as unsolicited admissions.[45] Later genuine requests from the police for information became part of an interview,[46] in the said case police officers investigating a burglary case came across wraps of papers and asked the appellant about them, the questions and answers became admissible although no caution was given and have to wait until that point where the officers had reasons to suspect the Suspect of any drug related offence.

---

40 *Amachree vs. Nigerian army* (2003) 3NWLR (PT.807) 256a 272-280 C.A; *R vs. Fulling* (1987) 2ALLER 65 at 691 (19770 Q. B. 426 AT 432.

41 *State vs. Jimoh Salawu* (2011) 12 S.C Pt.113, *R vs. Priestly* (1967) 51 Crim. APP. R.1; *Namsoh vs. State* (19930 5NWLR (PT.282) 144 (a) 179

42 Dennison M. et.al. 1990 Crim. L.R. 190 C.A.

43 *Rv. Mathews* (1990) Crim.L.R. 190 C.A.

44 *R. v Maguire* (1989) 90 Cr. APP.R.15

45 *R v. Scott* (1991) Crim. L.R.56

46 *R.v. Marsh* (1991) Crim.L.R. 455

This controversy about when interviews can said to have begun for the purpose of administering caution and suspect's safeguards was laid to rest by the Notes for guidance 11A of PACE which defines an interview as the questioning of person regarding his involvement or suspected involvement in a criminal offence or offences.

Note 12A stated that the aim of an interview is to get an explanation of the facts from the individual involved and not necessarily an admission. In *Maguire*[47] *and Marsh*[48] the level of suspicion elicited by the police towards the commission of a crime determines when an exchange becomes an interview. In *Weeks*[49]once exchange becomes interview the facts gotten earlier will have a retrospective effect on later exchanges and if safeguards applicable to an interview were not available in respect of such exchanges they will be excluded from evidence.

1992 Peace Model of Interview

Psychological science has in recent times influence the training of police officers and their interviewing practice, making it fairer and more transparent.[50]Prior to 1992, investigators in Britain did not receive official training in respect of investigative interview leading to high profile cases and miscarriage of justice in some cases, such as the Guildford Four and the Birmingham Six. PEACE is the first published national training program for police officers.[51]

Types of Interviews

a. **Question and Answer Approach:** This is a situation whereby the interviewer asks questions from the suspect about the topic of interest during the interview. The police usually have the information but the suspects may be in control of some other sources of information;

47 ibid
48 ibid
49 The Times, May 15, 1992
50 Fisher R.P. et.al 1992 Memory Enhancing Techniques for investigative interviewing. The Cognitive Interview Charles C. Thomas. Springfield U.S.A.p.15
51 Ibid

hence, the police need to explicitly ask if the suspect has anything else to add.

b. Interrogative Approach: Question and answer interview characterized as an asymmetric discussion between an interviewer and the suspect in which the interviewer dominates the discussion. It may involve implicit or explicit threats and coercion.[52]

It is found that this is the approach in Nigeria. The limitations include:

a. The risk of adversely influencing the suspect's mental state.

b. It improves the anxiety of an individual.

c. It raises the uncertainty of some people and they will doubt what they have experienced.[53]

d. Suspects looks for signals from the interviewer that their answers are acceptable and that their discomfort is almost over.

c. Persuasive Interview Technique: The religious faith of the suspect is appealed to and the suspects' is left without a choice of two decisions both of which are incriminating, rapport and a relationship is established making the suspect to feel an obligation towards the investigator and increasing the likelihood of confession. This method has the risk of producing false confession.Inbau.*et.al* suggests that these techniques should be used only when the police is convinced of the suspect's guilt because not all persons suspected of an offence are eventually guilty of the offence. Stephenson*et.al*[54]examining 1,067 police cases found out that the investigating police officers were certain of guilt of

52 Gudjonsson G.H. 2003. *The Psychology of interrogations and confessions* : A handbook

53 Ibid

54 Stephenson G.M et.al 1993 Attitudes and assumptions of Police officers when questioning criminal suspects. Issues in Criminological and legal psychology, *Crime & Law Journal* No.18.pp30-36

suspect in 73% cases prior to commencing the interview while in the United Kingdom, out of 4,244 people arrested and detained in 2007/2008, 411 gave false confession. The problem facing the Persuasive method is that information relevant to an investigation that identifies other suspects or incriminating the suspect may be missed while using the technique.

d. **Ethical interview**: This is an open –minded way of getting information, suspects are treated with respect and allowed to exercise their rights, and example of an ethical interview is PEACE. It is different from other methods not only because suspects are shown some measures of respect, but they are equally treated well during interview and investigators empathize with their situation. In most cases, interviewers were not very competent at the use of the approach.[55]From 400 video recordings and 200 audio recordings of police interviews reviewed by Baldwin, the investigators struggled to create rapport but find it easy to use the confrontational approach. The confrontational and confession seeking approach was mostly applied by investigators in 118 police taped interviews examined by Moston *et. al,*[56] particularly where the suspect remained silent or showed resistance or denied the allegation, interviewers frequently moved on to persistent repetitive questioning, ignored the suspect or closed down the interview.

---

55 Baldwin J. 1992, Videotaping police interviews with suspects- an evaluation (Police Research series paper 1) London: Home Office;1993 Police interview techniques- establishing truth or proof? *Criminology*,36, 109-134.

56 Moston et.al 1993. Police questioning techniques in tape recorded interviews with criminal suspects. *Policing and society*, Vol3 pp223-237

According to Stephenson et.al,[57] where the facts of the offence against the suspect is strong, interviewers used the confrontational method of extracting confession early in the interrogation process, where however, the evidence is weak, there were more likely to use the information gathering approach which produces a far better result of getting a confession.

The Miranda Warning

Miranda warnings are statutorily provided for by the 4th, 5th and 6th amendments of the American Constitution to ensure fairness before any custodial interrogation or questioning. It goes thus: You have the right to remain silent

- Anything you say can and will be used against you in a court of law
- You have the right to speak with a lawyer while being interviewed.
- If you cannot afford to employ a lawyer, if you want one, it will be assigned to represent you before any question.
- You may at any moment stop answering questions
- Do you comprehend the explanation of each of these rights?
- In view of these rights, would you like to speak with us now?

In America, the exclusionary rule operates to prevent the police from abuses and the courts from excusing such misconduct. *Mapp v. Ohio* makes it obligatory for courts in the country to apply the exclusionary rule, the rule is seen in some parlance as a necessary safeguard against police misconduct while some viewed it as an arbitrary measure which handcuffs the police. It actually fulfilled the need for efficient enforcement versus individual rights and freedoms.

---

57 Section 10 (a & b) of the Charter, 1982,

Other Jurisdictions

In other jurisdictions like the Northern Ireland, the Northern Ireland Act is in operation, Scotland has the Scotland Criminal Procedure (Scotland Act) 1995, amended as the Criminal Procedure and investigation Act, 1996, and it has a Code of practice. Apart from the Police and Criminal Evidence Act 1984, England has the Criminal Justice and Public Order Act, 1994, which recognizes rights to Silence, while a jury can draw adverse inference from the accused's relying on evidence not mentioned to the police at arrest. There is also the 1992 PEACE model of interview. Police and Justice Act 2000, Criminal Justice Act 1982, The Extradition Act, 3003 (police powers) order 2003, Police Reform Act 2002, Criminal Justice Act 2003, Police and Justice Act 2006 and Criminal justice and Police Act 2001.

In Canada, the Canadian Charter of Rights and freedoms entrenched in the Constitution prescribed the Charter rights and the caution rights before interrogation. There are also first and second police warnings administered to prevent any future statements from being admitted.[58] The first warning is that the suspect is not obliged to say anything as such in proof against him; the secondary police warnings are intended to inform the suspect of his right to have a counsel without delay and to be notified of his rights. They also serve to ward off the influence of any police officer offering any hope of benefit or, in the first place, to suggest any fear of prejudice to the suspects, including the present interrogator and warning that the suspect is not compelled to speak or say anything. The fact that suspect had earlier made a statement, does influenced the making of another statement. Video recording is influential as it correctly reflects the

---

58 Law Enforcement (powers and Responsibilities) Act 2002 (NSC); The Police powers and Responsibilities Act 2002 QLD, The Criminal investigation Act 2006 (WA), The Police Administration Act 1978 (NT); Crimes Act 1958 (Vic), Summary Offences Act 1953 (SA) and the Criminal Law (Detention and Interrogation) Act 1995.

interview room atmosphere in which the interview is conducted. An oppressive setting or investigator's threatening behavior is a good ground for inadmissibility.

The interrogation plan is prepared through a review of the profile of the suspect, criminal record, and past investigation, full details and elements of the offence being investigated is put into perspective for determination of when the suspect should be charged for the offence; possible defence like, motive, opportunity are examined and physical evidence analyzed to prove the suspects involvement. This is to prevent a suspect from providing an explanation to minimize their participation in the crime and surrender in the face of overwhelming proof.

Australia

In Australia, the scenario is somewhat comparable to that of Nigeria as caution is not statutory for long-term arrests or detention. The common law is the only major regulator of police interviews and it was vague and patchy, complemented by likewise vague and incomplete Judges Rules. The instructions or guidelines from the Police Commissioner is also used for dealings with suspects. The Crimes Act 1914 represented a trend towards codification of the rights of arrested persons and the requirement to be informed of those rights. The amendments of 1991 include rights of caution, not to say anything, and right to contact a friend, relative or lawyer with similar legislation in all states and territories.

Hong Kong

Hongkong has the Rules and Directions for the Questioning of suspects and the taking of statements, (Rules and Directions) of 1992. Caution rights are given whether a suspect is taking into custody or not and as quickly as a police officer has proof that would provide reasonable grounds to suspect that an individual has committed an offense. There are two gazette versions of the caution statement in English and in Cantonese and a suggested Putonghua version. Nigeria has a version only in English and it's not posted on any wall in our police stations.

New Zealand

New Zealand has a multilingual document on caution, legal assistance is given only in the interest of justice and if the person has no sufficient means. A practice note on police questioning issued by the Chief Judge of New Zealand in 2007 is with instructions of informing suspects of their rights.

Zimbabwe

In Zimbabwe, the Constitution and other statutes govern the right of a detained person.[60] By section 50 persons arrested must be permitted immediately at the expense of the state, to contact a legal practitioner and at their own expense to consult privately with a legal practitioner of their own choice. It is very essential to fairness of the trial in that if a suspect is denied this right, the suspect is deemed to be prejudiced in their defense and right to fair trial. In the case of a violation, suspect can bring an urgent application compelling the police or such agency to allow access to his lawyer. Zimbabwe law also permits the use of the trial within trial in determining admissibility or otherwise of a confessional statement. In spite of these procedural safeguards, pre detention rights are still flouted, and the police do engage in the acts of torture. Counsel however are permitted to interview suspects in private, without any police officer present and legally entitled to be present when statements are recorded contrasting with the case in Nigeria.

Singapore

Singapore has the Penal Code (amendment) Act no. 51, 2007.People could be arrested for 40 days before being officially charged. The privilege of self-incrimination and the presumption

---

60 Constitution of Zimbabwe; Amendment (no. 20) Act 2013

of innocence is not practiced, while law enforcement officers are justified in using any method.

South Africa

The Constitution of the Republic of South Africa, Bills of Rights guarantees certain fundamental rights that are protected in all conditions even for those under arrest.[61]This right requires them to give their names and addresses and to be notified of the effects of silence at that stage because their statement will be used as evidence against them in a court of law; they have a right to be charged to court within 48 hours while Section 35(4) requires that when giving information, it should be given in the language the person understands.[62] Section 35 (5) states that evidence obtained in a manner violating rights must be rejected in trial if it would render the trial unfair or defeat the administration of justice. Other rights include to have a lawyer assigned to the detained person by the state and at the expense of the state; detention rights consistent with human dignity, including at least the exercise and provision of adequate accommodation, nutrition, reading materials and medical treatment at the expense of the State and not to be isolated and visited by the spouse, partner, next of kin, religious counselor and medical practitioner selected.

2014 to 2015 witnessed increase in civil claims of wrongful arrest, detention and police brutality against the South African police amounting to R26 billion in damages. Other claims include revenue loss for victims for time spend in the police custody, medical / hospital expenses, general damages for pain and suffering, loss of support for an accused persons dependent and if the accused person dies during arrest and detention.

61 Section 35 (1) (a) of the South Africa Constitution.

62 Section 35 (4)

5

THE CONCEPT OF PRIVILEGE AGAINST SELF-INCRIMINATION

The privilege against self-incrimination protects the dignity of person whether free or incarcerated. This concept has its origins in the Jewish tradition with the maxim *nemoteneturprodereseipsm,* the principle that precludes coercing a person to accuse himself publicly.[1] The adversarial or accusatorial system of criminal justice administration speaks of a forensic contest between the state and the accused person during trials heavily contested to resolve dispute between parties.[2]Fundamentally conceived in England and in the United States,[3] its essential mainstay is hinged on the right to silence.[4] In large measure, its vitality and advantagesdepends on the protection of suspects' right to silence with counsel on both sides saddled with the task of determining the issues, presenting witnesses and proof on each side.[5] The state bears the onus of proving a case by means of witnesses and other facts to preserve the accused person's presumption of innocence.[6]

Effect of the adversarial system, particularly in the administration of justice was well captured in *Udo vs. The State.*[7] Following the ratio in *Gideon v. Wainwright,*[8] the court is of the view that a poor

1. Stefan A.R 1949 Law making and Legislative Precedent in America Legal History,33 *Minn. L. Review* 103, 118 (1949)
2. Ademola O.O 2013 Significance of an accused person 's right to mandatory legal representation in Capital Offence, *Ibadan Bar Journal. Vol.5 no.70-90, 71*
3. The 5th Amendment to the U.S Constitution which provides that No person "shall be compelled in any criminal case to be a witness against himself"
4. *Tehan v. United states* ex rel. Schott (1966) 382 U.S, 406,414
5 *Ibid.*
6 Gregory N. O. 1994 - 1995 England Limits the right to silence and moves towards an inquisitorial system of justice, *Journal of Criminal law and Criminal* 402 Vol.85, Iss.2,419.
7. (1988) 3 NWLR (PT.82) 316. supra at P.340, per Oputa, J.S.C 8 372 U.S 335

person who cannot afford to get the services of a legal practitioner cannot be treated fairly at trial. As a result of which the Government has risen to the assistance of indigents who are not financially capable to hire a lawyer in their defenses as they can consult the Legal Aid Council and the office of the Public Defender in some states to defend them. The legal aid lawyers available is however is limited in view of the teeming populace, increase in crime rate, funding and in respect of type of cases statutorily allowed under the law. The right to counsel is very fundamental and essential to fair trial in most countries including Nigeria.

Without the adversarial system of justice, the onus would have been on the accused person to establish his case and compelled the accused to testify in court during the trial. Indeed, a mere charge would generate a presumption of guilt while a judge or jury could pronounce the witness guilty, a procedure that could promote undue dependence on confession by the state to prove guilt by extrinsic means as criticized by Justice Goldberg.[9]

There have been many moves against the extraction of involuntary confessions, for example, China by way of developments of its legal framework Hong Kong passed the Bill of Rights in 1997 and also has the Rules of Directions for administering the caution and treatment of persons in custody in HongKong in 1992, without force of law. Ashworth[10] discussing the incorporation of the European Convention on human rights in the English law and the Human Rights Act of 1998, observed that the vast majority of significant decisions under the 1998 Act in criminal proceedings is about fair trial guaranteed under Article 6. Article 3 provides for the right not to be subjected to torture or inhuman or degrading treatment while Article 15 provides that the derogation of the rights is not permitted under any circumstances. Decisions in *Condron and Condroun v. United Kingdom*[11] is on point that adverse inferences may and may not be drawn from silence which is very influential.

9 1964 (378) U.S ,478, 489[1]
10 Ashworth A. 2001, Criminal proceedings after the human Rights Acts *The Criminal Law Rev.* 855-925 p. 868
11 (2000) 31 EHRR 1

In spite of the above decision of the court, stark conflicts of judicial authorities exists and severe disputes of power over the extent of the privilege against self-incrimination; since the House of Lords' decision in *R.v. Hertfordshire County Council, ex.p Green Environmental Industries ltd.*[12] It was not an issue for determination at all by the Privy Council in *Brown v. Stott*[13] and the latter decision has now been overtaken by contrary decisions of the Strasbourg court.

The question on whether the compulsion to speak creates a balancing away or takes away from the essence of the rights of silence and self- incrimination is debatable. It was held in *Brown v. Stott* that neither the right nor the privilege is absolute and the decision that contrary inferences may be drawn from accused person's silence was taken in *John Murray v. United Kingdom.*

Nigeria is not a member of the European Convention of Human rights, but has ratified about 400 other conventions and protocols[14] which until enacted and domesticated, it cannot have the force of law.[15] This is unlike under the English human Rights law wherein victims of human rights can litigate and appeal their rights, the story is different in Nigeria even with the advent of the Anti – Torture Act of 2017. There is however the National Human Rights commission set up in 1995 to see into human right abuses, working in collaboration with a number of NGOS. It has examined countless complaints but has been criticized for its in accessibility as well as not been able to redress human rights abuses. There are also investigations into human rights violations in Nigeria dated to June 14, 1999 and then recently Panels of inquiries and restitution

12 (2000) 2 W.L.R 373

13 (2001) 2 W.L.R.817

14 Procedure 1502, ECOSOC for women rights, UNESCO, ILO procedure, AU, ACHPR, E.U guidelines, OECD, ICC, ICCPR, UN, CAT,

15 Section 12 of the 1999 Constitution

to victims of Police abuse set up in some states as triggered by the End SARS protest of 2020.

The English case of King v. Warickshall[16] established the rule of exclusion of unreliable confession in court as opposed to credible confessions, the Court indicated that a proven, freely and voluntarily obtained confession deserves the greatest credit because it is derived from a guilty person and becomes the evidence of the crime to which it relates; but a confession gotten under undue influence of torture or fear is in a questionable form and should not be regarded as proof of guilt that no credit should be given to it.[17] Ibraheem in his study of confessions in criminal proceedings agreed with this and other decisions of courts as held in plethora of cases that confession is highly regarded particularly when proven beyond reasonable doubt.[18]

Cottrerrel Posits that the creation of confessions in terms of evidential value are strongly affected by police occupational outlook and authorized discretion, setting standards for compliance with the extant law.[19]

Odunsi in a study carried out in 2011on the significance of confessional statement in criminal trial discovered that confessional statements are responsible for over 60% of prosecution during trial yet little attention is given to its making owing to benefits of speeding up conviction and rewards of promotion to the investigating officer. There is also the problem of forensic investigation, analysis of ballistician, dearth of police laboratory and fingerprint database.[20]

---

16 (1783) 168 Eng. Rep. 234(K.B)

17 Ibraheem, O. T. 2013 the Relevance of Confessions in Criminal Proceedings. *International Journal of Humanities and Social Science* Vol. 3 No. 21 :291

18 *Osun v. State* 2012 Vol. 6-7 Pt. II MJSC 1; *Mustapha Mohammed v. The State* (2007) 11 NWLR (Pt. 1045) 303

19 Cottrerrel R. 1992 *The Sociology of Law: An Introduction,* 2nd ed. Butterworths. 284.

20 Odunsi, B. 2011: Criminal Law, Disease Control and HIV/AIDS Contextualizing Some Challenges of the Nigerian Criminal Justice System

The privilege against self-incrimination has its origins amongst the Judeo-Christian tradition, in the form of nemoteneturprodereseipsm which gives no room for individuals to make self-accusation under compulsion. The abuse and unfair treatment of suspects by the police during interviews and interrogations are the causes of the false statements in criminal proceedings.[21] The remedy proffered by the existing laws in Nigeria is by way of exclusion in court which is the current remedy for a confessional evidence obtained by overzealous Police during investigation. The Miranda rules in the United States of America,[22] the Police and Criminal Evidence Act 1984 and its Codes of practice operates in England and the Evidence Act 2011 in Nigeria are rules in these category. The interrogation room and what transpire there is still shrouded in secrecy.

Olatunbosun *et.al* opined that right of silence though entrenched into our constitution is not totally accepted, thereby resulting in low legitimacy. Consequently, victims of police torture and abuse do not appeal for redress as the right to silence is not actually understood within traditional norms. Also there is a lot of noncompliance by the police immediately after arrests and during the taken of the evidence of confessional statements.[23]

Ani, exposed the inadequacy of the provisions of Section 35(3) of the 1999 Constitution in respect of notification of the facts and grounds of suspect's arrest or detention in writing within twenty-four hours (and in a language he understands) and there is no constitutional provision for who to communicate the acceptance, rejection or lack of understanding of the right by

21 *NIALS Journal of Criminal Law and Justice*, Vol. 1.1-29.9

21 *Brown vs. Missisippi*, 297 U.S.278 (1936), the accused person was convicted on confession secured after whipping, by the U.S Supreme Court. *Miranda vs. Arizona* (1966) U.S.384.456 essentially provides that prior to any custodial interrogation or questioning initiated by law enforcement officers after a person is taken into custody or otherwise deprived of his freedom in any significant way, he must

22 be warned that he has right to remain silent.

suspects which is responsible for the importance ascribed to the right by the Police.[24]

Reilly,[25] supports presumption of innocence and privilege against self-incrimination under the United States' Fifth Amendment to the Constitution.[26] According to him, limiting the right is not good for an accusatorial system as it removes the defendants' cloak of presumption of innocence like in an inquisitorial system and transfers the onus of proving the guilt of an accused person with the calling of witnesses. This position is supported by the Covenant on Civil and Political Rights, 1966 which support the right not to be forced to testify against oneself or confess guilt.

Mill[27] proposed that the innocence silence at interrogation are justified and curtailment of this right will increase the probability of false confession and misconduct. Several reasons have been put forward as reasons for silence of a suspect during interrogation including protection of friends, family, sense of bewilderment, embarrassment etc. It is not however without its criticism of the right being advantageous to terrorist during interrogations.

Northern Ireland Rights to silence was limited in 1988 to while arresting terrorists, adverse inference would be made if an accused person failed to make account of suspicious objects carried on their persons and purpose at the location of crime. Has curtailing the right and the use of adverse inferences reduces crime? Testing the assumptions that a substantial proportion of criminals were ambushing the court trial by generating a fresh defense, Roger Leng, worked on 848 samples of police interviews gathered between the period of two years, found that 4.5 percent kept

---

24 Olatunbosun, A. 2012 Criminal Justice in Nigeria, Solerad Publishers, Ibadan.71

25 Ani C.C. 2011 Reforms in the Nigerian Criminal Procedure Laws: *NIALS, Journal of Criminal Law and Justice.* Vol. 1. 54-93

26 Reilly, G. 1994-1995, England Limits Rights to Silence and moves towards inquisitional system of Justice 85 *J. Criminal L.A. & Criminology* Vol. 85 no. 2, 402-452

27 The fifth Amendment of the United States Constitution provides that no person shall be compelled in any criminal case to testify or be a witness against himself.

quiet during questioning, meaning that the exercise of the right was small and by creating a fresh defense, a substantial amount of criminals ambushed the court trial.[28]

It was also observed that real ambush defense is very uncommon and when raised, only about 50% were effective. Empirically information is lacking on the assertion that the right is commonly taken for granted by detainees or impedes prosecution of criminal conviction. In reality, the study found that the right to silence would improve opportunities for convicting culpable offenders. Mcconville *et.al* however concludes that the right to silence should be reinforced rather than further weakened or diminished as it has been found that police officers use silence selectively when interviewing suspects.[29]

Stein[30] rationalizes 5th Amendment of the U.S. Constitution protecting innocent defendants whose evidence has no corroboration in court.[31] According to him if the right is limited particularly for simple offences, guilty suspects would group with the innocent by making false statements. Where the innocent finds it difficult to support and corroborate their statement with credible facts, he will naturally be classified with the guilty a trend that is damaging on an innocent defendant and society as a whole.This minimizes the pooling effect of suspects whether guilty or not, resulting in fewer innocents being convicted more than a regime where the right is curtailed. In effect it minimizes wrongful conviction.

---

28 Hirst, J. 1993.Royal Commission Papers a policing perspective; Police Research Series, Paper 6. *The right to silence in police interrogation: a study of some issues underlying the debate,* Study 10, Leng.R. Ed. Gloria LayCock, Home Office London. 35

29 Hirst J. 1993.The Royal Commission Research Papers, a policing perspective; Police Research Series, Paper 6, Study 16, *Custodial legal advice and the right to silence* McConville,M. et al. & Study 19. *Crown Court Study* Zander M. and Henderson P. 19. Ed. Gloria Laycock, Home office London.

30 Stein, A. 2008 The Rights to silence helps the innocent. A Response to Critics, *Cardozo*

31. *Dickerson vs. United States* (1994) U.S 530, an attempt to abolish the Miranda Rules by Congress was declared unconstitutional.

Burke et al, interrogated 1,227 suspects after the curtailment of the right was suspended, only Six percent invoked the right compared to ten percent prior to the abolition of the right. Ten percent in addition did not answer compare to 13% under the regime of right to silence a decrease was observed in the proportion.[32] A study by the Royal Commission further shows that silence does not affect reduction of cases that police investigate, increase acquittal in court and it does not increase the use of ambush defence.[33]

Baldwin performed a survey to limit the right to silence by studying 400 videotaped recordings, 200 audiotape recordings, 1% did not answer, while 18 percent were silent. The Royal Commission discovered in a study conducted on whether right to silence leads to unjust acquittal, out of 490 suspects, 79(16%) cases were dropped at pre- investigation, 54(11%) was dropped by the Prosecution, 25 (5%) acquitted by a Jury at a contested trial and 12% remained silent. It concluded that adverse inference would not increase convictions or reduce crime.

Rogers[34] noted that most suspects do not understand the nature of their rights while in custody including their Miranda rights and the constitutional safeguards even after the decision of the court in the Miranda's case. In a survey about Miranda warnings completed by 119 students in a college and 149 pretrial defendants at Jails in Texas and Oklahoma, 36% students and 31% defendants incorrectly thought that their silence could be used in a trial as incriminating proof.

---

30. Stein, A. 2008 The Rights to silence helps the innocent. A Response to Critics, *Cardozo Law Review*, 1116, vol. 30; 3.
31. *Dickerson vs. United States* (1994) U.S 530, an attempt to abolish the Miranda Rules by

32 Burke T, et.al 2000. The Rights to silence: impact of the Criminal Justice and Public Order Act 1994, 110
33 *Ibid*
34 Rogers R. 2011. Rights to Remain Silent not understood by many suspects, proceedings of 119th convention of the American psychologist Association. Retrieved from American psychological Association Site on 2/2/2016.

Rogers in an empirical study further discovered that having a legal representative helps the right.[35] Only 11 percent of the interviewees who had legal representatives were silent during interrogation, whereas in 78 percent of instances in another research by Rogers in Study 16, legal practitioners did not advice silence which corroborates the fact that in 80 percent of instances silence was not based on legal advice. It was found out that interview witnesses like the responsible adult for juveniles usually leave them unprotected from police interview tactics, they rarely intervened, ignoring the use of the right of juveniles.[36]

In *Salina vs. Texas*[37] the Supreme Court in a 5-4 ruling concerning a noncustodial suspect, ruled that the right is no longer what it is. In that case, Salinas was invited to the Police station, he was not arrested nor was his Miranda Rights read over to him. Two of the judges believed that Salina had no right to invoke before the detention. In that situation, Justice Breyer disagreed that a person who is not a lawyer may not understand the specific phrases of invoking the privilege against self-incrimination. He proposed a far better way of inference of exercising the fifth Amendment's privilege from silence and surrounding circumstances.[38]

In Nigeria, though constitutional, the suspect's right to stay silent is exercised more during the trial and not during interrogation.[39] After arrest, a person's right of silence is constitutional and should be immediately applicable, and he cannot be forced or coerced to

35 Hirst J.1993; Royal Commission Research Papers; A Policing Perspective. Paper 6, *The conduct of Police interviews with Juveniles.* Study 8. Roger Evans. Ed.s by Gloria Laycock Home Office Research Group

36. *Ibid*

37 (2013) 570 U.S In that case, Ernesto Miranda was convicted for kidnapping and raping in 1963. While in police custody, he made no request to consult with counsel while being interrogated, but was also not advised by the police that he has right to do so. At trial, his confession was rejected by the Supreme Court on the ground that Police had failed to comply with a set of rule governing interrogations that were made for the first time.21.

38 Ibid.p.7

39 *Igabele vs. the State* (2006) 2 SCNJR, 129.

say a word unless he volunteers to do so, it cannot also be made a subject of prosecution' comment.

Sections 35(2) and 36(11) of the Constitution raises no ambiguity on the right of suspect to silence during police investigation. However, the effective interpretation and application of these provisions are seriously in doubt since judicial authority has revealed that these Constitutional provisions would not protect the accused person in court, thus accused person is obliged to say what he knew about the allegation leveled against him otherwise it will amount to admission by conduct.[40] Also, it has been said in some parlance that the provisions indirectly gives judges power to infer from the silence as observed in the case of *Salina vs. Texas*, [41] even though prosecution is barred from making any comment to that effect. The right is therefore not really effective after all in protecting a suspect if exercised whenever criminal allegation is made against him.

Furthermore, the entrenchment of these Constitutional provisions has not stopped an average Policeman from obtaining involuntary confessional statement through the instrumentality of all sorts of inhumane treatment, torture or inducement.[42] It merits mentioning that the Nigerian Courts commend the police for applying Judge's Rule[43] as a desirable practice but where, however, same is not applied, such cannot vitiate the confessional statement because it is a mere rule of administrative procedure and not mandatory.[44]

---

40 Ibid

41 Ibid (2013) 570 U.S, 178

42 Section 39 Evidence Act. (2011), *Basil Akpan v. The State* (2007) All FWLR (Pt.351)1578-C 1579.*Okeke v. The State* (2000)10 NWLR (Pt.675)423 at 437; *Dotun Fatilewa v The State* (2007) All FWLR (Pt. 347) 719. *Akpan v. State* (2001)15 NWLR pt.737)748.

43 *Abubakar v. The State* (1969) NSCC 6.

44 Fakayode E. O 1977.The Nigerian criminal code companion, Ethiope publishing Corporation, Ibadan, .111

Chin[45] opines that words of caution should be clear for the avoidance of self-incrimination as understanding of the words depends on factors like culture, the environment, peer pressures and interactions between suspects and interviewees. Reasons for excluding involuntary confession is given by Lord Griffitus as unreliable confession and that no one should be compelled to self-incriminate.[46]

Discussing the Questioning Code and its revision, Wolchover et al, opined that the practical impact of the changes made in it with suggestions for further impact of informing suspect of the right to a solicitor is not available under the old code on first suspicion /arrest in the field, but there is for formal detention at the police station. According to him the old code and its amendment has little detail on notification to detainees about consulting a lawyer, though there is the length of notification for free legal advice. In the past, detainees declined the advice on the grounds that they could not afford it. By the new code, every police station charging area must display posters on the right to legal advice and it is now a continuing right all through the custody period; therefore, even if you do not immediately access it, you can have it.

Clockars, while looking at the police's working culture, argues that the use of discretion is an accepted norm among the police which is necessary and essential for the exercise of police powers even when recording the suspects 'confessional declaration after arrest.[47]

45 Chin J.W.K. 2009 Criminal Interrogation and the Right to Remain Silent, a study of the Hong Kong Customs Service *International Journal of Police Science & Management Volume 11 number 2; State Vs. Olasheu* (2012) All FWLR (pt. 614) 152 where investigator says he "obtained" the statement from the defendant, then it is not voluntary. as the demand for the statement has rendered the caution useless.; *State Vs. MatiAudu* (1971) NNLR 91-92; *NakundeVs Jos* (N.A) (1966) NMLR in*Queen vs IGP,* (1957) NNLR25

46 *Lamchi-Ming vs. R* (1991) 3 ALL ER 172 (a) 178 (1991) 2 AC 212 at 220: *R vs. Mustaq* (2005) 3 ALL ER; A *vs. Secretary of State* (2006) ALL E.R. (575).

47 Klockars C.B. 1985 *The idea of Police,* Beverly Hill; 6th edition. Calif: Sage. Publisher Incorp.

Fieldman examines Judges' search for principled consistency in relation to procedures affecting the rights, welfare, detention and interrogation of suspects under the PACE Codes. According to him, Judges have two weapons by which they give force to decisions about the proper operation of the Act and Codes by way of exclusion of evidence which would have been relevant and admissible and delivering of rulings on admissibility of confessions.

Birch[48] examining the operation of the English Police and Criminal Evidence Act,1984 which is in Pari materia with Sections 28 & 29 of the Nigerian Evidence Act 2011, observed that a prosecutor seeking to adduce evidence must overcome three hurdles. The first is Section 76 (1) which appears deceptively jumpable, while subsection 76 (2) provides for grounds of challenging admissibility upon oppression and unreliability.[49] However, the confession would be excluded if its admission will adversely affect the fairness of the proceeding.[50] For him, exclusionary laws serve to be disciplinary for misconduct of the police that occurred during the interrogation phase. It is regarded as safeguarding most fundamental rights of the suspect by stopping the prosecution from deriving any evidence-based advantage from the infringement, whether accidental or intentional.

He sees oppression as having to do with what was said or done by the police in the interrogation process. The rationale is to express the unacceptable nature of the intentional misconduct of the police and to dissuade its repetition by excluding the evidence thus acquired. In other words a regulatory approach to exclusion. Non-compliance attracts discipline of erring officers as mere exclusion

---

48 Birch D. 1989 The Pace Hots Up: Confessions and Confusions under the 1984 Act*The Criminal Law Review* 95; *Matto vs. Wolverhampton Crown Court,* (1987) R.T.R.337.

49 Section 76(2) (a) & (b) of the Police and Criminal Evidence Act, 1984.

50 Ibid Section 82 (3).

of the evidence may not be enough to uphold suspects' rights as it automatically leads to exclusion under the Act. He observed that they are breaches outside the definitions of oppression that are in the same category as wrongful, impropriety or sheer wickedness where the rules of interrogation are broken and rights of suspects infringed.[51]

Stuntz believes that a confessional statement obtained under coercion should not only be excluded by the court where the right governmental structure and policy is in place but should serve to deter erring officers and protect suspects' rights.[52]

Leo et.al,[53] describe confession as false where a suspect admitted to a crime that has not occurred and there are enough proofs to show that the defendant may not have been engaged in the act or omission.

Mirfield[54] while defending tape recording suggested that government should try to develop an enabling system that increases public confidence about the accuracy of record. It defines proof of confession as uncommon in that it is usually obtained by authorities who anticipate that it may be used in criminal proceedings at the moment. According to him, tape recording reduces the prejudice to the accused that puts his credibility in issue by challenging the Police. The question however is that at

---

51 *R v Davison* (1988) Crim.L.R.442, Central Criminal Court, *Hughes* (1988), Crim.L.R.545; *Samuel* (1988) 2ALLER.13 on the right Legal advice.

52 Stuntz W.J. 1989 The American Exclusionary Rule and Defendants' Changing Rights *Crim. L.R* 117-128.

53 Leo R.A et.al. 1998 The consequences of false confessions; Deprivations of liberty and Miscarriages of Justice in the age of psychological interrogation 88- *J.Crim l. & Criminology*
429,449

54 Mirfield P. 1984 The Future of the Law of Confessions *Crim. L.R.* 63 Tape recording was first introduced in 1972 by the Criminal Law Revision Committee and in January 1981, the Royal Commission on Criminal Procedure introduced routine tape recording gradually under administrative guidance from the home office.

what stage should the recording start? Is it at the point of commission of the crime? Is every conversation recordable? What should be tape recorded? Are all crimes to be recorded? What is the nature of the equipment and in what environment? In a soundproofed room? Failure to record, does it lead to exclusion?[55]

Lassiter et.al,[56] in a study conducted discovered that while tape recording is useful to prevent coerced and aggressive use of interrogations techniques, perspectives of recording is important as wrong perspective can be misleading and possibly be an inadvertent tool for injustice.

In Scotland, confessions are allowed to be recorded outside the

station.[57] It is a fact that videotaping can fail as a result of many factors including, suspects' refusal, equipment unavailability or failure. Other circumstances include those common in Nigeria such as incessant power supply, unavailability or unsuitability of the interview room, play back of recording and time wasting.

Onadeko O.[58] posit on the provisions of Section 15 (4) of the Administration of Criminal Justice Act,2015 that confessional statements may be electronically recorded on a retrievable disk or on such other audiovisual media. According to him, there are no provisions in the Act for the category of devices or gadgets for visual recording of statements, safekeeping and other eventualities that may occur in the process of recording. He further observed that participants at a recent workshop on effective execution of the ACJA 2015, recommended the use of officer's mobile device.

---

55 *Tanner* (1977) 66 CR. App.R.56.

56 Lassiter G.D. et.al. 1986 Videotaped confession: The impact of Camera point of view on judgments of coercion. *Journal of Applied Social Psychology* Vol.16 pp. 268-276, presented at the Eastern Psychological Association, Baltimore Lassiter G.D.et. al. (2006) Videotaped confessions: Panacea or Pandora 's Box. *Law& Policy Journal*, Vol. 28,192-210;

57 *McCormille and Morel* (1983) Crim.l.R.150.

58 Onadeko O. et.al 2016; An appraisal of the attitude of the Courts to the Administration of Criminal Justice Act 2015) *Miyyetti quarterly Law Review Vol.1 (issue1)*,.9-31

This is in a quest for how to make the provision functional and he also suggested the tying of officer's promotion to ACJA to ensure compliance.

Sebastine O. at the Nigeria Law Reform Commission (NLRC) at a workshop on the reform of the Public Officers Protection Act,[59] observed that the development of law to curb police violation of an accused person's right is gradual, unmonitored and contains no provision for remedy or compensation to a teeming populace comprising of ignorant and uneducated suspects whose rights in this area are being violated on a daily basis.[60]

Akinseye-George examined the use of words like "May be" and "police officer" used in Section 15 (4) of the Administration of Criminal Justice Act, 2015. To him, electronically recorded statements has made the use of this technology optional coupled with the peculiarities of the Nigerian environment where this equipment might not be readily available in every police station.[61] The use of Pen and paper recording of statement in Nigeria, being the conventional way is greatly challenged by the availability of the writing materials at our police stations which has made permissible the culture of collection of money from suspects to record their statements.

Coughlin[62] postulates that Confessions arise from an investigator/ criminal cooperation whereby the interrogator encourages the suspect to talk until the admission of guilt. She is of the view that interrogations have strategies for questionings for various offence.

---

59 Cap. p.41, Laws of the Federation of Nigeria, 2004,

60 Sebastine SAN et.al. Recommendation to the Nigeria Law reform Commission (NLRC) at a workshop on the reform of the Public Officers Protection Act, CAP P41, Laws of the Federation of Nigeria, 2004.

61 YemiAkinseye-George 2016, Issues on Criminal Justice Administration in Nigeria, *Prosecutorial Standards and the evaluation of Evidence under the Administration of Criminal Justice Act.2015* Eds. Adedeji Adekunle *et.al*

62 Coughlin A.M. 2009 Interrogation stories; Victim blaming in the contemporary interrogation room is firmly entrenched in the contemporary law in 2004 as in the early 1960. *Virginia Law Review* vol.95, no.7, 1599-1661

For instance, blame stories are told in instances of rape to make the suspect to confess. Confession at least from the suspects' perspectives provide access to the entire tale.

Hambali[63] is of the opinion that police pre-trial investigations often naturally throw up quite a number of incidence of which confessional statement is amongst and unless handled within the requirements of the law, may affect the trial of a suspect which in the long run may bring injustice. According to him, interrogation of suspects by overzealous police officers with little regard for the extant laws coupled with police reliance on discretion makes such process vulnerable to miscarriage of justice.

Bodede[64] opined that the cultural background and peculiarity of Nigerian factor and the fact that suspects are illiterate and uneducated have not helped the situation. According to him it is impossible and impracticable to require in the case of primitive and unintelligent accused person's evidence, the administration and the understanding of necessary caution before making of a statement.

Ochem discussing confessional statement in criminal trials in Nigeria observed that confessional evidence must be corroborated to prove its veracity. It is not aimed at determining whether the accused made the statement, this is determined by the judge in his fact finding capacity at the end of the case, whether the statement is voluntary and therefore admissible.[65]

Drizin *et.al*[66] discovered that 84% of false confessions happened after more than six hours or longer interrogations and that the average length exceeded 16 hours.

---

63 Hambali. D.V. 2012 Practice and Procedure of Criminal Litigation in Nigeria , Seat print and Publish Limited, lagos Chapter 2. 81

64 *Ahmed Vs. The State* (1999) 5 SCNJ 223.

65 Ochem, C.M.2011,the Relevance of confessional statement in Criminal Proceedings in Nigeria, *Igbinedion University Journal of Jurisprudence & Public Law* Vol.1, no.2,2011 p.23

66 Drizin, S. A. 2004 The problem of false confessions in the post-DNA world *North Carolina law review*, vol. 82, 891-1007.

Kassin *et al.*[67] discussing the Reid technique and blame shifting method, opined that police helps the guilty to escape; with police like this, who needs a defense lawyer? Police privilege one narrative after the other until the victim succumbs against possible alternative narrative. Interrogators identify a psychological state and pick it up for a criminal responsibility defense.

Basil examines some methods and techniques of interrogation commonly used in Nigeria like the File and Dosier technique, we know all technique, Futility technique, Rapid fire technique, Matt Jeff or friend/ foe technique, Incentive technique (for stick and carrot) technique, Repetitive technique, Pride and Ego technique, Silent technique and change of scene technique. Also there are basically four stages of conducting interrogation, the rapport building stage,and information exchange stage, challenging stage and ending.[68]

A 2010 study was conducted by the John Jay College of Criminal Justice at CUNY that used laboratory experiments to assess how the bluff method correlates with the confessions of innocent parties. The bluff method indicates to the suspect of the possession by the police of evidence that they do not actually have, with pressure applied to force innocent people to make confession.

One of the most significant results in guilt manipulation as indicated in police interrogation manual is that the interrogator may achieve a state of guilt in the suspect which may spring from a different source entirely.[69] Report from the Innocence Project gives an approximate rate of 25 percent being numbers of exonerated convicts that actually admitted to the commission of a crime,

---

67 Kassin, S.M et.al. 2003The psychology of confessions: A review of the literature and issues. *Psychological science in the public Interest* .Vol.5. 35-69 Sage Publisher.com

68 Basil M. 2013 *Law, Rules and Procedures of Criminal Investigation in Nigeria* Evergreen overseas publications limited. 101

69 Gudjosson, G.H, 2003, *The Psychology of Interrogation and Confessions: A Handbook* ; John Wiley& Sons Ltd England,7

They suggested 12 hours for interrogation and any confession acquired in excess should become inadmissible and those of more than six hours should only be admissible if the prosecution is able to establish that they were voluntary.

Ani,[70] describes torture as a feature of police interrogation in Nigeria with the main objective of obtaining confessional statements from the suspects a situation that exists despite the provision of Section 34(1)(a) tha tno person shall be subjected to torture or to inhuman or degrading treatment and Section 8 (1) of the Administration of Criminal Justice Act, 2015. According to him, the sections domesticates Principles for the Protection of all persons under any form of detention or imprisonment.[71] This principle is supported by Article 1(2) of the United Nation's Declaration on the Protection of All Persons from being subjected to Torture and other Cruel, Inhuman or Degrading Treatment or punishment.

Ajulo,[72] sees Administration of Criminal Justice system in Nigeria has being outdated, overdue for reforms, largely infertile and loose. According to him, provisions of the law that seeks to prohibit inhuman treatment of an arrested person or torture has always been respected on paper and not in practice. According to him, gross violation of this particular fundamental right of an accused

---

70 Ani C.C. 2011 Reforms in the Nigerian Criminal Procedure Laws: *NIALS, Journal of Criminal Law and Justice.* Vol. 1. 54-93 op.cit.14

71 Principle 1 that all persons under any form of detention or imprisonment shall be treated in a humane manner and with respect to the inherent dignity of the human person. Adopted by General Assembly Resolution 3452 (xxx) of 9th of December, 1975. Defining torture as any act by which severe pain or suffering, whether physical or mental, is intentionally inflicte the instigation of a public official on a person for such purposes as obtaining from him or a third person information or confession, punishing him for an act he has committed or is suspected to have been committed, or intimidating him or other persons. It does not include pain or suffering arising only from, inherent in or incidental to, lawful sanctions to the extent consistent with the standard minimum Rules for the Treatment of Prisoners or suspects, torture constitutes an aggravated and deli berate form of cruel, inhuman or degrading treatment or punishment.

72 Ajulo K.2014, Observations & Recommendations on the proposed Administration of Criminal Justice Law in Nigeria; *The Jurist, Law Review on contemporary Legal issues in Nigeria,* A Publication of Law Student Association of Nigeria, Uni Abuja. 197

person is usually carried out covertly. He suggested proper documentation of custodial interrogation of an accused person which must be properly documented and recorded. In particular, visual and audio recording should be from beginning to the end and all interrogation must be with the written authorization of a most superior officer. In a 2011 research, it was reported that Nigeria has no tradition of systematic forensic analysis, only a single ballistician, one police laboratory and no fingerprint database throughout the nation.

In the Miranda case, the court noted that there is secrecy and gap in our understanding of what actually goes on in the interrogation rooms. Useful data on current police practices could only be gleaned from numerous Police Manuals and textbooks that document past successful processes and suggest numerous efficient strategies. It is however not uniformly guided. This speaks volume of the use of discretion in the exercise of Police Powers.

Boswell[73] states that each story's value depends on its being true of an image of either a person or a human nature in particular, if it is incorrect, it represents nothing. Bluhm legal clinic[74] have further revealed that what is presented to prosecutors by the police as confessional statement are often obtained by lying to Suspects, for instance, Kevin Fox after 24 hours detention and exhaustion and 8 hours of questioning was told that his wife has ceased to believe him and his family to love him; implicit promises of leniency that if the suspect admits the guilt he will not be charged. It is also suggested in some parlance that a reliability test or trial within trial should be made a subject of pre- trial proceedings rather than being conducted by a jury or a judge as the case may be in an emotional laden Court-room proceedings.

73 Boswell, J (1970) *Life of Johnson* 685 R.W. Chapman ed. Oxford Univ. Press. 1799.

74 On wrongful conviction sees 2015 declared as a momentous year of world false confession; Retrieved Sept 3rd 2015 from Http//www.law North Western Law.

Kassin,[75] classifies false confessions into three stages; voluntary false confessions, usually sacrificial and without the promptings of the police. A parent may admit the guilt of an offence for instance, to save their kid from prison or for attention purposes. In 1947, about 60 people confessed to the 1947 murder of Elizabeth Short also known as the black Dahila.

Compliant false confessions are provided to prevent stressful situations, prevent penalty, earn a promise or implied reward. A police interrogation room that has no windows but only a table and two chairs could create severe mental exhaustion for a suspect who may admit guilt of offences they have not committed in order to escape. Offer of coffee, what looks like interrogation cessation, can trigger false confessions as a consequence of extremely suggestive interrogation techniques.

75 Kassin S.M. 2011 Current directions in Psychological Science

6

SUSPECT'S RIGHTS IN CRIMINAL JUSTICE SYSTEM

Rights to Silence

The concept of the Rights to silence stems from the human right perspective recognized by history and most Constitutions of countries including, The Magna Carta of England of 1215, The United States Declaration of Independence 1776, The French Declaration of the rights of man and the citizen 1789, The American Bill of Rights 1791, Universal Declaration of Human Rights 1948, other Declarations and Constitutions of many countries.[1] Human right is universal, it connotes the right which a man enjoys and share with his fellow men, whether suspect or free. These rights are supportable by both natural law and positive law antecedents. Naturalist notably Locke, Rousseau, Aristotle, Black stone, John Rawls, Robert Nozick are generously in agreement that the state of nature was one of perfect liberty,[2] in which man was free from the constraints of the organized political society or systemized legal system and so men by nature have right to liberty. The legal systems of many countries recognize the existence of at least some absolute human rights and protect them through enshrinement in the constitution, one of the rights is the right to silence.[3] It is however expected that no circumstance or emergency justifies government infringing the interest protected by some rights.[4] Historically right to silence began from the West from the

1 Article 1, Universal Declaration of Human Rights 1948: All human beings are born free and equal in dignity and right. Article 5: The right to freedom from torture.

2 Akinseye –George Y. 2011, *Judicial protection of Human Rights pub. Centre for Socio –Legal Studies,* Abuja, Nigeria Marvellous Mike Press ltd. p.9

3 It is a right that exist prior to any legal system and any legal system which does not recognize them as unjust.

4 Elegido J.M. 1994 *Jurisprudence: A Textbook for Nigerian Students* Akinola Aguda, Ed. Spectrum Books ltd, Ibadan, Chap. viii pp. 177-178

17th to 18th century for religious and political protections and later suspects and accused persons in criminal cases. Basically, the right prevents an individual from standing up in challenge alone against the State and it is also significant for the presumption of innocence.

Miranda warnings and others like it are found in many jurisdictions consisting mainly of right to silence and legal advice. It has more to do with fair administration of justice than with getting the truth. Suspects and accused person has the right not to answer any question until after consultation with a legal practitioner or any other individual of his choice.[5]Once a formal charge has been lodged it would be unreasonable to remain silent in the face of it. An accused person has no burden of proving his innocence and is not required to say anything before or during the trial. During police interrogation, an accused person is not compelled to say anything, making it compulsory to administer caution for all suspects before police interrogation. In any criminal trial, the accused is not compelled to provide proof. However, it is not in all instances that an arrested or detained individual is silent when alleged of a crime for being in a state of apprehension with an endangered freedom, an average person would naturally react to an allegation of a crime.

Section 35(2) of the 1999 Constitution provides for the right to silence and presumption of innocence and requires that any individual arrested or imprisoned shall have the right of silence and not answer any question until legal advice is sought from a lawyer or other persons. [6]Section 35(3) of the constitution offers that detained should be notified of the facts and reasons of his arrest or imprisonment in writing within twenty-four hours (and in a language he understands)[7]. These constitutional provisions in

5 Ibid Section (36)(2)

6 These rights, where contravened is justiciable; Section 45(6) (1) of the 1999 Constitution.

7 Chapter IV of the 1999 constitution of the Federal Republic of Nigeria.

conjunction with Section 6 of the ACJA guarantee a suspect's right to silence before trial. The essence is that a suspect must be prevented from self-incrimination before he or she is formally charged.

The right echoes the maxim *nemodebetprodore se ipsum* (no one should be forced to betray himself) The right to silence is very key to the guarantee of other rights built round it, it comprehensively protects suspect from self-incrimination, guarantees that he has legal representation and the making of his confession statement willingly and not under compulsion or force. Therefore, the police have the duty not only to warn a suspect of his right to silence at the moment of arrest, but also to ensure continuous and adequate access at every stage of interrogation to counsel. This is also in line with the ACJA's purpose of section 17(2).

The outcome or waiver of such right the suspect makes in respect of right to silence and counsel and who records the outcome is not however captured by the law. The mode of compliance is not captured even for ACJA, apparently this has encouraged the nonchalant attitude of the police on whether or not the right was properly administered during the arrest.

Section 491 (1) of ACJA provides that where no other sanction is provided for in this Act, the failure by the suitable officials to discharge their responsibilities under this Act without reasonable cause shall be regarded as misconduct. This provision appeared to be like medicine after death because by the time a noncompliance is detected, the affected suspect would have been unjustly or unfairly treated as there is no provision in the Act for how to report the unfairness or oppression of the police. This researcher who is a deputy director in the Ministry of Justice observed from participant observation method that in most cases, accused persons having been traumatized may not even have an understanding as to who to report or file a report to. The occupational culture of the police is a hitch that will prevent them from approaching the police or report one colleague to another.

In Nigeria, the law extend the right to silence to trial of criminal cases. It is however exercised more during trial and seldom respected during interrogation.[8] The right as provided by the law should be applied as soon as an arrest is made and should progress into interrogation without force or being coerced to say a word, whatever happens at the investigation shall never be a subject of comment.[9]

Marrying Section 35 (2) of the Constitution with Section 36 (11) means that a suspect or an accused person has the right to be silent both at investigations as well as in court. The said sections are unambiguous but its application is doubtful in respect of its effectiveness in application and the protection it offers suspects/ accused persons in the face of incriminating allegation as allegation leveled against an accused person needs to be refuted immediately, otherwise it will amount to admission by conduct.[10]

In some parlance these provisions of the Constitution as mentioned earlier has somewhat empowered the court to infer from the silence of the accused person as observed in the case of *Salina vs. Texas,* [11]and in *Daniel Sugh v. The State.*[12] The Supreme

8 *Igabele vs. the State* (2006) 2 SCNJR, 129

9 Section 35 (2) of the Constitution of the Federal Republic of Nigeria, 1999.

10. Section 181 of the Evidence Act 2011.

11. Ibid p.22. The accused had a Phillipino woman with whom he was cohabiting. The woman also had another man as her friend. The accused and that other man were struggling and quarrelling with each other as each of them wanted to have the woman to the exclusion of other. On 17/10/08, the woman and the man were being driven in a bus with a few other passengers along Makurdi-Gboko road in Makurdi town when the accused forced the bus to a halt and inflicted injury on the deceased with cutlass. The deceased was qu ickly rushed to the hospital but was later certified dead.

12 10 (1988)5SCNJ58

Court held in the latter case that by section 33 (11) of the 1979 Constitution an accused person cannot be compelled to give evidence at trial. In this case however the suspect having been arrested and while giving statement to the police, the accused person said he reserved his statement until he had seen his lawyer. The accused was sentenced by the court on the ground that the accused did not include the details he later talked about in court in his earlier statement to the police.

The courts have rightly maintained in plethora of cases, that the constitution is a living or organic document, hence Human rights provisions should be interpreted in such a way that their very essence or effectiveness is not impaired. It should be seen as practical and efficient, not illusory. Making an adverse inference after the right has been exercised merely suggests a strategy that removes with the left hand from what was provided with the right hand.[13] In essence, all human right are core, one is not above the other and therefore indivisible, interdependent and interrelated.[14]

As earlier stated the rights of suspect to silence is hinged on section 35 (2) of the Constitution of Federal Republic of Nigeria, 1999,[15] the Administration of Criminal Justice Act, 2015[16] and Administration of Criminal Justice Laws in states that have enacted it into law including Anambra, Ekiti, Oyo and Lagos states etc.[17] The right is constitutional, recognised under our jurisprudence and further strengthened with the innovation of the video recording of the statement of a suspect. Under the ACJA and the ACJLS laws, suspects should not only be informed of the right, but where they choose not to exercise it, it should be recorded to avoid abuse. The essence is to prevent a suspect from self-

13 *Awolowo v. Usman Sarki Minister of Internal affairs* (1960) 1ANLR 178 PP.18

14 ibid

15. As amended.

16. Section 6 (2) (a)

17. Section 3(1) Lagos ACJL 2007 (as amended, 2015). Rights to free Legal representation from the office of the Office of the Public Defender, Legal Aid Council or any such Agency. As at May, 2018, 15 states have enacted the ACJL.

accusation without formal charge.[18] It was found that interrogations conducted in isolation is unfair while coercive questioning vitiates the confessional statement when obtained within such an interrogation process.[19] The fact however remains that the rights to silence has the effects of reducing crime and helps to control abuse of state powers.[20]

Under the English law, it was found that the right is rarely used by suspects because from samples of 848 police interviews in a study from 1986 to 1988, only 4.5% invoked their rights to silence due to the samples environment, while an insignificant number of criminals were found ambushing proceedings during trial with a new defence and 50% successful when raised. [21] The right was therefore more regularly used by suspect who have access to a legal practitioner. The reason is that the right exists in theory more than in practice while responsible adults are usually passive in intervening against police pressure and self-incrimination.

In practice, the right is also seen as been advantageous to the guilty, hamstringing the police with legal status that are not clear cut and concise. Admission by conduct otherwise known as the drawing of adverse inference is common at trial as there is no law to the contrary save as under Section 236 (1) (c) of the Criminal Procedure Code. It is found as a matter of fact that the police though need a little persistence to execute their task of detection and solution to crimes makes use of high handed methods. The rights of silence prevents self-incrimination of oneself, its curtailment may not bring any significant changes to reduction of crime.

---

18 Adekunle A, et.al 2016. Recording of statements made by suspects: A Review of Section 17 of the Administration of Criminal Justice Act, 2015: *Issues on Criminal Justice Administration in Nigeria:* 122- 144.

19 *Haynes vs .Washington* (1963) 373 U.S 503

20 Burke, T. et al.2000. The rights of silence, The Impacts of the Criminal Justice and Public Act, 1994 Home office Research study.

21 *Op.cit*.p. 83

22 10(1988)5SCNJ58

At pretrial and during trial, the right is difficult to sustain, this is because the guidelines are not clear as to what the investigation officer should do or refrain from doing. In *Daniel Sugh v. The State,*[22] it was held that Section 33 (11) of the 1979 Constitution is a provision against compelling an accused person to talk in a criminal trial because the accused person having been arrested by the police said he reserved his statement until he had seen his lawyer. He was later convicted on the ground that he did not include what he said in his statement to the police. It was contended on appeal that failure of the appellant to make a statement immediately on the happenings that resulted in the death of the deceased eroded his right under section 33(11) of the 1979 Constitution. The appeal was refused and the Court observed that the accused simply reserved his statement until he had seen his lawyer, what he later said at trial should have been written in his statement to the police which was his first opportunity to explain what happened. The court further observed that under normal circumstances of human behavior, an accused person by way of instinct would deny an allegation and will want to offer an explanation capable of justifying, defending or establish his or her innocence from any guilt than to remain silent and wait for another time to do so. In this particular case, there was an eye witness at the scene of the crime.

In *Adekunle vs. State,*[23] the accused did not immediately gave reasons for firing a gun, not even an explanation at cross examination that it was an accidental discharge. It was observed by the Court of Appeal that the accused person no doubt has the right to remain silent at his trial and the prosecution has the burden of proving his guilt beyond reasonable ground, he must however speak and defend himself early enough to put up a defence of accidental discharge. In *Utteh & Anor v. The State* it was held that

22 10(1988)5SCNJ58

23 S/C 30th of June, 2006. Per. Ikechi Francis Ogbuagu.

the accused person is not bound to say a word as he has the right to silence while the prosecution proves his guilt beyond reasonable doubt.[24]

Decisions under the European Convention on Human Rights indicates that the right is limited.[25] In *John Murray v. U.K* for example,[26] the European Court of Human Rights has pronounced that the rights could be infringed and yet justifiable. Drawing of adverse inferences is allowed and it might reasonably be drawn in situations where the accused person should have explained, this is so as long as conviction was not based solely or mainly on such inferences. This position was supported by the Judicial Committee of the Privy Council in *Brown vs. Schott*[27] which established that the right to silence and privilege against self-incrimination are not absolute.

By Article 6 of the English Human Rights Acts the right being a right at the heart of fair procedures, appears unrestrictive on the face of it, but as judicially interpreted, it is not really absolute. *In Saunders v. United Kingdom*[28] the court observed that a violation of the privilege might be justifiable. In the midst of the debate for balancing of rights, proportionality, essence of silence and self-incrimination, it is summed up that the exercise of a victim's right should not extinguish the very principle of the defendants' right. No restriction, not even public policy or interest, inconsistency in the law or case laws should destroy the very principle of the right.

---

24 *Utteh & anor vs. The State* (1992) 3NWLR (pt.138)

25 The European Convention on Human Rights is an international treaty to protect human rights and political freedoms in Europe. It came into force on the 3rd of September, 1953 and is in its 60th years of existence, The court set up in Strasbourg to deal with violations of the European convention on human rights has reached well over 10,000 judgments in cases such as that brought by Natsvlishvil prompting changes to National laws and procedures in nearly 50 countries. In 2011, U.K. was found against for lack of effective investigation and failing of duty twice of non-prohibition of torture. https://www.the guardian.com visited 17/8/18.

26 1996, 22 E.H.R.R.29. PARA 47.

27 2001, 2 N.W.L.R 817.

28 1997 23, E. H.R.R.313, at paras 69 and 74.

Whether proportionate to any public interest or not, *Heanney and McGuiness*[29] makes this clear that any pressure on an accused person to speak, is not good for the exercise of the right as it rendered it ineffective, given subtle silence approach to police interrogation is disadvantageous to a suspect.

In the U.K, suspects' right to silence is fettered under the Criminal Justice and Public Order Act 1994,[30] under interview , a suspect can no longer keep quiet as that will work against the suspect whose failure or refusal to talk as soon as possible, will be used against him in court. It is however different where the suspect was deny his right to legal advice or right to a duty solicitor under the law before being interviewed, charged or informed that they may be prosecuted; and have not changed their mind about wanting legal advice.[31] The type of caution given to be given when restriction applies also differs. The assertion that it gives significant unfair advantage to criminals and accused person who uses the right to avoid possible charges is not backed by any systematic empirical evidence to support that view. The benefit is also considered as low to the proportion number of suspects charged, the level of pleas and convictions.

That the right is being abused by the guilty suspect or that it impedes prosecution or conviction of offences is also unfounded. In fact, suspect's denial is more effective in hampering police investigation than silence. The advantages of the right is more than that of its limitations or removal which would enhance the prospects of convicting guilty offenders in only a very small proportion. The Right need to be reinforced and not otherwise

---

29 2001 Crim. L.R.481

30 Section 34, 36 & 37 of the Criminal Justice and Public Order Act, 1994 (CJPOA) are not sufficient without additional evidence to establish a case to answer or a finding of guilt.

31 Annex C , PACE Codes

to avoid selective use of the right during interviews of suspects under investigation.[32]

Findings also revealed that the right prevent the guilty criminals from pooling with the innocents as they will not be able to make a defensive statement, which gives the guilty an alternative to lying and opportunity of the truth to be discovered in the course of lying. In essence, right to silence serves the innocent more than the guilty.

The study further discovered that silence in a person often means innocence and at other times means other reasons like, confusion, being naturally silent as a person or lack of understanding of the words of caution.[33] It is more effective in practice where the extrinsic evidence available to law enforcement agents and prosecutors are intermediate and the evidence is neither here nor there in strength. Right to silence has no effect where evidence is strong, prospects of conviction is high and the evidence is clear and positive, pointing to the guilt of the accused person. In cases of weak inculpating evidence, the innocent and the guilty stand the chances of being released. It serves the innocent more than the guilty by reducing the rate of wrongful conviction.[34]

Access of suspects to a legal practitioner

The right is guaranteed under Section 35(2) of the Constitution which provides that any person who is arrested or detained shall have the right to remain silent or avoid answering any question until after consultation with a legal practitioner of his own choice. It is the most fundamental constitutional right for a suspect as the

---

32 Annex C , PACE Codes C

33 Hirst, J.1993. Royal Commission Papers a policing perspective; Police Research Series, Paper 6. *Custodial legal advice and the right to silence* Study 16, McConville, M.et.al. 33; *Crown Court Study,* study 19 Zander, M. and Henderson, P. 34 Ed. LayCock, G. Home Office London.

34 Steven Greer. 1990 The Right to silence , a review of the current debate ; 53 *Modern law review,* 709

counsel protects the client's rights and assemble the evidence necessary for a determination of his guilt or innocence[35]; without it a suspect risk torture, threats, duress and conviction.[36] In *Adebesin v. The State,*[37] the essence and purpose of legal representation was given as protecting the rights of the accused person. It also helps officers to comply with the law for which they risk civil suits under the Fundamental Enforcement proceedings for violation of suspect's constitutional rights. Failure to provide this right would render the statement obtained without it inadmissible and unconstitutional.[38]

The provision resonated in the Administration of Criminal Justice Act, 2015 which provides that the police officer or the person making the arrest or the police officer in charge of a police station shall inform the suspect of his right to remain silent or avoid answering any question until after consultation with a legal practitioner or any other person of his own choice. Subsection 6, 2(b) as well provides that the suspect consults a legal practitioner of his choice before making, endorsing or writing any statement or answering any question put to him after arrest.[39]

Flowing from the above mentioned provisions of the laws, there is no other provision of the law, rule or regulation on how to guarantee or monitor the practicability of the enforcement of these rights. For instance, if the suspect should be notified of his right to legal advice; who communicates the information to the suspects? If there is a waiver of the right, who records it? Where are the lawyers to give legal advice during arrests? Police officers

35 Eruaga, A. 2018 Rights of silence of crime suspects is an unnecessary clog in the wheelsof justice, Retrieved on 20th of October/10/18 from https:// en.m.org Wikipedia.

36 Legal advice is one the most important and fundamental right of a citizen Per Hodgson J. in *Rv. Samuel* (1988)

37 Section 58 of PACE 1984

38 (2014) 9 NWLR Pt. 1413 at 60

39 *Olushola v, A.G Federation* (1982) 3 NCLR.895

care less about the importance of these rights being of the view that the rights are not so very important[40] and an indigent, illiterate suspect oftentimes may find it difficult to get the services of a legal practitioner.[41] It was found that there are no provisions or measures to ensure compliance, to detect noncompliance and to punish violations of the right. The right to consult a legal practitioner is expected to be available in the laws for application prior to questioning and interrogation.

Section 6 (2) (c) of the ACJA provides for free legal representation, but can a lawyer forced on a suspect be regarded as the suspect/ accused person's choice? What if he doesn't have a choice because of his financial condition? An indigent suspect may not really have a choice in respect of a counsel assigned to him by the Legal Aid council or the State. In *Udofia v. State*[42] counsel assigned to an accused person from the legal Aid Council was absent without tenable reasons over and over again during trial as a result of which the Supreme Court ordered a retrial. The Court in *Idiang v. State*[43] held the view that the Legal Aid Counsel should start to be a bit discriminatory about counsel they brief, certainly not counsel who have no interest in the matter nor counsel who could not assist this court. The fact also remains that the Legal Aid Council Act 2011 does not cater for all offences. Counsel from that office can only take up cases of Murder, Manslaughter malicious or grievous hurt, assault, common assault and affray.[44] As at 2012, the Public Complaints Commission concluded 825 cases and 290 others were at different stages of investigation while the Legal Aid Council, with its problem of underfunding as stated by the Director-General in 2007, cannot provide adequate representation

40 Subsection (2) (c) free legal representation by the legal Aid Council of Nigeria where applicable. Section 18 of the ACJL, Oyo state, 2016.

41 Gudjonsson, G.H. 2003. *The Psychology of interrogations an confessions a Handbook,* Wiley ed. Graham Davies & Ray Bull pg.9 "Do not make a big issue of advising the suspects of his rights, Do it quickly , do it briefly and do not repeat it"p.17

42 *Oyakhere v State* (2006) all FWLR PT 305 (a) 716 C.A

43 (1983) 3 NWLR, part 84,p.533

44 (1981) N.S.C.C. 273 at 274

for suspects who get in touch with a lawyer for the first time after having been charged to court under a withholding charge at the Magistrate court.

In *Arogundare v. The state,* [45] the accused person was convicted on an oral version of his accounts of killing his father to an Asst. Comm. of Police on routine visits to suspects who confessed to him at 2.a.m in the night. The accused person was convicted because the confession was so graphic, and vivid that its veracity is not in doubt, there was no corroboration, and no autopsy. As at when the confession was made, there was an isolation and no legal advice. It was found that the provisions on confession in the Evidence Act are important as it originates from the constitutional rights of silence rooted in the maxim *nemo tenetur seipsm accusare hence* the need for proper consultation with a legal practitioner before the writing of statements,

In *Awolowo v. Usman Saraki, Minister of internal Affairs*[46] the right of a litigant to a counsel of his own choice was interpreted restrictively to mean counsel of his own choice who could enter into the country as of right as a result of which the litigant was deprived of representation by counsel meaning that the accused person's Counsel of choice means a legal practitioner that could enter the U.S. as of right which defeats the spirit of the right to legal counsel.

Under the PACE Codes C, detainees must be told of their rights to consultation and communication to counsel privately at any time whether in person, in writing or by telephone with availability of a free legal and independent advice.[47] Interestingly, legal representation helps suspects to use the right and not otherwise. It was observed in a study that only 11% suspects out of those

---

45 Section 8 (2) of the Legal Aid Act, 2011.

46 (2009) 6NWLR (pt.1136) 165.

47 1966, 1 ALLNLR 178,18

with legal advice were silent at interviews,[48] 78% suspects got no legal advice, 80% had legal advice yet were not silent. Interview witness like the responsible adult for juveniles, rarely intervened, leaving off the right of the juveniles unprotected and exposed to the police interview tactics.[49] The latter supporting the fact that it is only a legal practitioner that can really protect the right of a suspect at interrogation.[50]

The requirement of administering caution to a suspect.

A review of the laws and judicial dicta in Nigeria reveals inconsistency in the treatment of confessions that are not preceded by caution and the law. Judicial interpretation says non-compliance with the Judges rule without the use of caution have no effect on the admissibility of the confessional statement. The importance of caution is further whittled down by section 31 of the Nigerian Evidence Act, which provides that a confessional statement does not become irrelevant because it was made under a promise of secrecy or in consequence of a deception practiced on the defendant for the purpose of obtaining it or when he was drunk; because he was not warned that he was not bound to make such statement and that evidence of it might be given thereby, making the administration of caution of little or no importance.[51] Caution is important before the extraction of a confessional statement because it guides the suspect on what to say or write. This judicial interpretation to the importance of caution has further robbed off this constitutional right of being informed of rights to silence

48 Paras 6.1; No police officer should at any time, do or say anything with the intention of dissuading any person who is entitled to legal advice in accordance with this Code, whether or not they have been arrested and are detained from obtaining legal advice.

49 Hirst J. 1993; Royal Commission Papers a policing perspective; Police Research Series, Paper 6. The right to silence in police interrogation: a study of some issues underlying the debate. Roger, E. Study 8.Ed. by Gloria Laycock Home Office Research Group.30

50 Hirst J. 1993. Royal Commission Research Papers; A Policing Perspective; Police research series, Paper 6. *The conduct of police interviews with juveniles.* Study 10. Rogers, E. Ed.by Gloria Laycock Home Office Research Group; A Policing Perspective. Ed. by Laycock G. Home Office Research Group. 30.

51 Section 6 (2) (b)

and consultation with a legal practitioner of choice before being questioned found in most warnings and caution statement. The investigating police officer is quick to say the accused person volunteered his statement after caution when evidence shows that the statement was taken days and weeks after arrest.

This study found that in some jurisdictions the words of caution are written in the local language of that country for example Hong Kong[52] has translated caution words from English into Cantonese language and a suggested Putonghua version. The two languages are also gazzetted. Nigeria has a version only in English and it is not or never posted on walls in the police stations. New Zealand has a multilingual document on caution stating that legal assistance is given when the interest of justice requires it and the person has no sufficient means.[53] In the United Kingdom caution is statutory and it is given when there are grounds to suspect an offence before any questions about the offence is asked or further questions if the answers provide the grounds for suspicion.[54]

In the U.S.A, the Miranda warning has a semblance to caution which is constitutional. In *United States vs. Patane*,[55] it was held that the Miranda warning is for the purpose of protecting the defendant from harmful testimony. It is found that the procedures of caution are similar in the U.K and U.S, the Codes and Miranda warning have a force of law. Where a confession is found to be a coerced confession, occasioned by a harmful error, meaning affecting a constitutional right of the defendant, it is considered as a serious error it is never regarded as a simple error, but technical one and thus must be excluded.[56] Under PACE, consideration for exclusion

52 *Akinmoju v. The state* (2000) 6NWLR (PT.662) 602

53 the Rules and Directions for the Questioning of suspects and the taking of statements (Rules and Directions) of 1992

54 A practice note on police questioning issued by the Chief Judge of New Zealand in 2007 has further instructions regarding informing suspects of their rights; the practice notes supplement the relevant statutes and do not change the existing law or prevent any judicial developments.

55 10.1 Paras C.56

56 *Arizona v. Fulminante* (1991) U.S. 279

are based on what was said or done; circumstances existing at the time of the confession; what was said or done in light of such circumstances that could likely renders unreliable any confession which might be made by him in consequence thereof; whether the confession was made in consequence of anything said or done or likely to have effect identified by.

7

LEGAL FRAMEWORKS REGULATING SUSPECTS' RIGHTS DURING EXTRACTION AND RECORDING OF CONFESSIONS

Chapter IV of the 1999 Constitution guarantees fundamental human rights of citizens whether free or in custody[1] it is significant for the purpose of maintaining the standards of freedom and prevent the often concealed invasion people's rights by the government.[2]Some of the rights includes silence, presumption of innocence and dignity of the human person.

By section 35 (2) of the constitution any person who is arrested or detained shall have the right to remain silent or avoid answering any question until after consultation with a legal practitioner or any other person of his own choice. Subsection (3) of that section provides that any person who is arrested or detained shall be informed in writing within twenty-four hours (and in a language that he understands) of the facts and grounds for his arrest or detention. Section 36 (5) provides for the presumption of innocence of every person charged with a criminal offence, until he is proven guilty while Section 36 (6) (a) provides for notification of the nature of charge to persons charged with a criminal offence in the language that he understands and in detail of the nature of the offence;[3](b) be given adequate time and facilities for the preparation of his defence; (c) defend himself in person or by a legal practitioner of his own choice. The rights cannot be curtailed in any form, in fact they are absolute. There is also room for payment of money and apology openly from affected authorities or quarters in case of unlawful apprehension or detention under Section 35 (6) of the Constitution.

---

1 *West African Examination Council V. Omodolapo Yemisi Adeyanju* (2008) NWLR. (PT.1092) ,270

2 Ajomo, M.A.1993, *The development of individual right in Nigeria's Constitutional* History; individual Rights under the 1989 constitution Ajomo & Owasanoye Eds. Nigeria Institute of Advanced Legal Studies p.

13 It has been observed that this provision of law should be more applicable at arrest and during interrogation of the suspect which is not so.

The only constitutional provision regulating false or coerced interrogations in the event of torture is found by Section 34 (1) (a) of the 1999 Constitution to the effect that every individual is entitled to respect for the dignity of his person and accordingly-No person shall be subjected to torture or to inhuman or degrading treatment.

The above provisions notwithstanding, it has been observed that torture is still a feature amongst other tactics employed by the police in the extraction and recording of confessional statement in Nigeria. According to Niki Tobi,[4] torture means to make someone passes through a form of pain or anguish, it is the bodily brutalization of a person, an inhuman treatment which is fierce, coarse and harsh with no human touch treatment.

There are no circumstances which justify the police or other law enforcement officers hurting or humiliating anyone using methods such as torture or subjecting them to beatings or other forms of violent treatment in order to make them confess; what is permitted is only a reasonable force which may be used to detain a suspected criminal who resists arrest.[5]

A national survey recently reveals the heart-rending conditions under which incarcerated persons in Nigerian prisons and police cell are kept. With this background information, it is not an exaggeration to say that with a custodial arrest of any individual in Nigeria, ill treatment resulting in infringement of their right is common place.[6]Section 35 (2) notwithstanding, right to silence is

3 It has been observed that this provision of law should be more applicable at arrest and during interrogation of the suspect which is not so.

4 JSC as he then was.

5 Ajomo, M.A, 1992 Fundamental Human Rights under the Nigerian Constitution proceedings of International Seminar on Human Rights, Lagos.p.5

6 Ibid.

daily impugned by psychological tactics of interrogation allowed by the police, thereby eroding this right. The reason is not farfetched from the inadequacy of the law and absence of more detailed constitutional provisions or code which makes the recording of response and waiver obligatory for the police particularly for suspects' choice to information about legal practitioner and silence. This is mostly responsible for the indifference of the police in administering the deserved legal rights to suspect during arrest and investigation.[7]

The Administration of Criminal Justice Act, 2015

The Administration of Criminal Justice Act 2015 hereinafter referred to in this study as the ACJA is a major reform to criminal procedure in Nigeria.[8] It is an adjectival piece of legislation which seeks to regulate procedural steps and processes towards ensuring justice. One of its purposes under focus here is protection of the interest of the suspect during interrogation which is of universal acceptance. The law reiterates the fact that justice should not dependent on the depth or shallowness of one's pockets but on the sense of doing justice to all parties concerned in criminal matters.

Section 6(1) of the law provides that except when the person arrested is in the actual course of the commission of a crime or is pursued immediately after the commission of a crime, or escapes from lawful custody, the police officer or other persons making the arrest shall inform the person arrested of the cause of arrest. Section 6 (2) (a)-(c) of the law further provides for the

7 Ani, C.C 2011. Reforms in the Nigerian Criminal Procedure Laws: NIALS, *Journal of Criminal Law and Justice* vol.1: 54-93

8 The ACJA, 2015 repealed the Criminal Procedure Act, 2004 and the Criminal Procedure (Northern states) Act, 2004, the Administration of justice Commission Act cap A3 LFN 2004 and the Administration of Justice Commission Act cap A3 LFN 2004, it however did not repeal the Criminal procedure Code Act, Cap 491, LFN, 1990.

interrogation and recording of the suspects' confessional statement. According to these provisions, the suspect shall be notified of his right to silence or choice of not answering any question until after consultation with the legal practitioner of his choice or with any other individual of his choice; shall consult the legal practitioner of his choice before issuing, endorsing or writing any statement or answering any question placed to him after detention and free legal representation by the Legal Aid Council of Nigeria where applicable.[9] These provisions reiterates section 35 (2) of the constitution.

Evaluating the provision of the above mentioned section of the ACJA, it was observed that there is no additional provision for how the suspect would be immediately taken care of in respect of his rights and recording of his statement where the circumstances demand that such rights be administered outside the police station. There is limitation of the recording of statements to the police station alone even when certain facts may become distorted or lost if not recorded immediately or when delaying an interview would not only lead to the destruction of evidence, but people at risk and cause investigation trails to go cold.[10]

Is the right continuing? Should the suspect first be taken to the Police station before he is informed of his rights or should he be at the point of arrest? The laws are not detailed enough to accommodate these exigencies? The answer is not provided in the law. It is also observed that level of protection for suspects under the section is very minimal thus creating room for false confession. Under the original U.K. PACE Code before amendment, a suspect would be told that he is being arrested, the reason for the arrest and will be interviewed at a police station and

9 Ibid. Section 3.

10 Agbonika, J. et.al 2014 Delay in the Administration of Criminal Justice in Nigeria: issues from a Nigerian view point *Journal of Law, policy and Globalization. Vol. 26*

not before arrival. The custody officer then informs the suspects of his rights at the police station. Specifically only exposed person interviewed outside the police station will demand for a legal advice.[11]PACE Code C also allows the HSE interviews outside the police station and not necessarily will the suspects be detained or put under arrest.

Fenwick,[12]basing her observation on the revised codes of 1991 which is very elaborate,[13]distinguished between interviews within and outside the police station which cannot be labelled an interview but relevant to the offence. Interviews of suspects before police station are often subject to some prohibitions including practicable, contemporaneous recording of volunteer's statements. Within the police station, safeguards under Code C of PACE are applied.

The safeguards available within the police station include contemporaneous recording, tape recording, reading over, verification and signing interview notes and information of suspects about their legal right to a legal practitioner or appropriate adult before questioning. This procedure also applies to an interview within other premises and on the street interview. According to her, Paras. 11.3 of the old code[14]provided for only accurate record[15]and the presence of an appropriate adult which are loopholes for the police to abuse the right of suspects.[16]

Section 6 of the ACJA makes the consultation of a lawyer mandatory unlike the permissive regime of Section 352 of the Criminal Procedure Act[17]which makes provisions for counsel to an accused Person who faces a capital offence if practicable, an expression that appears restrictive,[18]making suspect's rights subject of judicial interpretation rather than statutory.

---

11 Code C, PACE: This right to urgent interview is not provided under the ACJA, the police officer or the person making the arrest must inform the suspect of his rights only at the police station, this could have well been at the point of arrest.

12 Fenwick, H.1993, Confessions, Recording rules and miscarriages of justice, a mistaken emphasis, *Crim. L. R.* 174-183.

13 The revised Code C has extended record for any interview irrespective of offence on whether or not the suspect has been arrested with a suitably compliant authorized recording devise, written interview or visual recording with sound.

14 Now Para 11.13, verifying and signing rules have been supplemented that a suspect should declare in his or her own hand, on the interview record that it is correct.

By Section 17(1) suspect's written statement may be made in the presence of a suspect's chosen counsel if he so wishes.[19]Where this is not practicable, an officer of the Nigerian Legal Aid Council (LACON) or a Civil Society Organization (CSO) or a Justice of the Peace (JP) official or any other individual could witness to the making of the statement.[20] An interpreter is to be given to a suspect who is not literate in English language, who shall then endorse the statement as having been made by him, [21]who shall attest to the making of the statement.[22] In *State vs. Gwonto & ors,* [23]it was held that the interpreter is important for ensuring that the suspect understands the trial proceedings and thereby enabling

---

15 Original Para.11.3 provided that if the interview took place in the police station or at other premises. "The record must be made during the course of the interview unless if in the investigating officer's view, this would not be practicable or would interfere with the conduct of the interview.

16 Unreliable confessions may most likely emerge from informal exchanges, (admissions from informal, level of suspicion chats, booking in charging procedures), mechanisms triggering off the main safeguards in Note 11A (interviews generally) and Paras 1 1.1(prohibition) are deficient both in creating large areas of uncertainty as to the level of protection called for at various points and in allowing the minimal level of protection under para.11 to operate in too many contexts

17 Section 186 of the Criminal procedure code is rather couched in mandatory terms.

18 *Osuolale V. The State* (1991) 8 NWLR, Pt. 212, 770.

19 Section 17 (1) ACJA, 2015

20 Ibid. Section 17 (2). 17 (3) For a suspect that does not understand or speak or write in the English language, an interpreter shall then endorse the statement as having been made by him and the interpreter shall attest to the making of the statement.

21 1983 3iLaw/ S, C.69/1972; *Sunday v. FRN* (2013) LPELR- 2019 2 (CA)

22 Section 17 (4) ACJA, 2015

23 (1984) 5N.C.L.R. 61

justice to be done. The suspect is not to be interfered with while he is making his statement; however, interference would be permitted where a legal practitioner is discharging his role as a lawyer.

This is perhaps a very fundamental right, since the existence of counsel protects the right of the suspect who may eventually defend the suspect if he is charged to court. The police have a general apathy towards protecting the rights of suspects, and in situations where it is administered, it is not properly done, hence the need for engaging a legal practitioner. Provisions of Section 6 and 17 of the ACJA bothers on establishing a standard for the protection of suspects from coercive acts of state officials charged with the obligation to investigate the crime and removing the culprit and the society from criminal acts.

Oyakhire[24] however observed that Section 17 does not have provisions for what happens when the suspect refrains from making a statement which could be in writing or oral,[25] and also, what happens if the suspect waives these rights. Also the section has been observed to be permissive and not mandatory, as having a legal practitioner in attendance during the taking of the statement is a matter of choice. There is also the challenges of choosing a foreign lawyer qualified to practice in Nigeria and requiring the permission of the Chief Judge of Nigeria. One envisages a situation whereby obtaining authorization may take time making the lawyer unavailable at the end of the day. Consequently, the option of engaging a member of LACON, CSO, JP or any person of choice though important, is subject to their availability too. The practicability of this is very questionable in that where the latter's choice fails, any legal practitioner could be given to the suspect and whose services may not be affordable or good enough.

24 Oyakhire, S.O.2016, Issues on Criminal Justice Administration in Nigeria, Eds, Adedeji Adekunle et.al. Recording of statements made by suspects: A Review of section 17 of the Administration of Criminal justice Act 2015, NIALS, 122-144, 125

25 Section 15 (5) ACJA

Eventually, the suspect may be left with none or at most any person of his choice who may not be knowledgeable about statutory rights of suspects. The danger in this is that it could promote a continuous detention of suspects which ordinarily should not have been more than one day or two depending on the situation.[26]

In addition to oral and the written confession being admissible in evidence[27] [28]the statement may be video or audio recorded.[29] This technology is advantageous in terms of providing room for the monitoring quality of the interview, scrutiny and guidance but only with proper training of officers. Lassiter[30]suggested that where police personnel are trained on perspectives and angles of recording in videotaping, it helps judges to make findings. This is because juries are overly influenced by confessional evidence which is the most incriminating[31] followed by eyewitness and character testimony.[32]Where videotaping is used, the perspective from which a confession is videotaped determines its voluntariness, which could be confession or interrogator focused. Trained police photographers are therefore needed to implement this technology so as to avoid bias and achieve the right focus. It has also been said to promote a less aggressive and coercive interrogation.[33] In Nigeria, the recording of confessional statement is still at his

26 Section 35 (5) of the 1999 constitution.

27 Section 15 (5)

28 Section 17 (1)

29 Onadeko. O et.al 20.16 an appraisal of the attitude of courts to the ACJA. *Miyyetti Quarterly law review* Vol. 1 (issue 1), June 2016.

30 Lassiter A.A Jennifer J. et al, Videotaped confessions: Panacea or Pandora's Box, 2006 *law& Policy Journal*, Vol.28, issue 2, Pages 192-210 April 2006

31 *Joseph Idowu v. State* (2000) 7SC (pt. 11) 50 @ 62,

32 Kassin & Neumann, 1997 Power of confession evidence and experimental test of the fundamental difference hypothesis randomized controlled trial. *Law hum Behav,* Oct.;21 (5) 469 -84

33 Daniel Lassiter et al. journal of applied social psychology vol.22. issue 23, Dec.1992 pages 1838-1851

elementary stage and there is need for guidelines towards the storage, retrieval, duplication, sharing and destruction of electronically recorded statements of suspects.

Regrettably, the use of the word "may be" or "police officer" in the ACJA in respect of the use of electronic recording of statements has made the use of this technology optional coupled with the peculiarities of the Nigerian environment where this equipment might not be readily available in every police station.[34]The use of pen and paper recording of statement in Nigeria, being the conventional way is greatly challenged by the availability of the writing materials at our police stations which has made permissible the culture of collection of money from suspects to record their statements. Mandatory recording is only available by Section 9(3) of the Administration of Criminal Justice Law 2007 of Lagos, which authorized the use of video or compact disks while recording a confessional statement. The said recording and copies then filed in court and produced at trial, where there is no device for the video, the statement shall be written with a legal practitioner witnessing.[35]

The procedure is further plagued with many challenges. Falana, noted that the provision is highly innovative and would likely minimize objections to the admissibility of confessional statement in criminal trials, however in jurisdictions like United States of America that is making use of electronic recording of statements trial within trial have not been eliminated. This suggests that videotaping or audio taping may not completely eradicate the

34 Yemi Akinseye-George 2016, Issues on Criminal Justice Administration in Nigeria, Eds. Adedeji Adekunle et.al Prosecutorial Standards and the evaluation of Evidence under the Administration of Criminal Justice Act.2015, 1-31, p.10

35 Section 18 (2) of the Administration of Criminal Justice law, 2016 of Oyo State of Nigeria; any person who is arrested with or without a warrant volunteer to make a confessional statement is recorded on video and the said recording and copies of it may be produced at the trial provided that in the absence of a radio facility, the said statement shall be in writing in the presence of a legal practitioner.

problem of coerced and forced confession.[36] The situation therefore calls for more efficient safeguards during interrogation so as to ensure accuracy, fairness and completeness.[37]

The ACJA is silent on the thorny issue of involuntary confession and this is of concern in that torture cases are on the increase all in a bid to extract confessional statement. In a study carried out by the Nigerian Institute of Advanced Legal Studies, 50% of the accused persons reported cases of police abuse.[38] The increase persists in spite of the extant legal provisions to safeguard torture and other international conventions supporting a total eradication of torture while handling suspects or persons detained in police custody. This includes the Body of Principles for the Protection of All Persons under any form of detention or imprisonment to be treated in a humane manner and with respect for the inherent dignity of the human person[39]and Article 1(2) of the United Nation's Declaration on the Protection of Persons from being subjected to Torture and other Cruel, Inhuman or Degrading Treatment or punishment. Torture is an act of austere pain or suffering, physically or mentally inflicted on a person by or at the direction of a public official so as to get a confession from him or from a third person after punishing him or her for an act committed or suspected of having been committed, or intimidating him or other persons. It is an intensified and intentional type of painful, callous or demeaning handling or punishment. The provision of Section 8(1) is an attempt to curb excessive police tactics by making provisions for humane treatment of persons arrested upon suspicion of commission of a crime.[40]

---

36 Falana, F. The Administration of Criminal Justice Act will ensure all law enforcement Agencies work together This day Newspaper November 9th,2015)

37 Ibid p. 16-17

38 Ajomo, M.A. et al, 1991 Human Rights and the Administration of Criminal Justice Lagos : Nigeria Institute of Advanced Legal Studies, Lagos .121

39 Principle 1 that all persons under any form of detention or imprisonment shall be treated in a humane manner and with respect for the inherent dignity of the human person.

40 Onadeko, O. et al, 2016 An appraisal of the attitude of Courts to the Administration of Criminal Justice Act 2015 *Miyyetti Quarterly Law Review*,vol. 1:(issue1) 9-27

The problem of involuntary confession have been of great concern to major stakeholders in the Justice sector it is however debatable whether the innovation about electronic videotaping of confessional statements has been effective to curb involuntary confession.[41]Section 15 (4) provided that confessional statement can be electronically captured on a video or audio tape, the type of device or gadgets for visual recording of statements, safekeeping and other eventualities that may occur in the process of recording is not adequately provided for by the Act. Officers' mobile device have been suggested in a quest for how to make the provision functional with tying of officers' promotion to ACJA to ensure compliance. This is in addition to other rights including rights to have a solicitor present or sitting in at interviews, to help give the suspect legal advice; advise him on his rights so as to ensure fair play at the police station and attending identification parade where necessary.[42]

The question of whether an offence has been committed is not always difficult for the Police, particularly in Nigeria. What is difficult is finding out who committed the offence? And due to factors like sheer incompetence, corruption, or blatant abdication of constitutional or statutory responsibility, the police forces out a confession from a no crime circumstance with sheer bullying, making suspects to admit what they did not do. With the availability of basic scientific tools, the police can unravel any difficult case without resort to violence on the suspects and witnesses.[43]

41 Ibid, p. 9 - 31 Section 15 (4) provided that confessional statement may be recorded electronically on a retrievable disc or on such other audio-visual means.

42 Holtham, J. 2005 *Criminal litigation, Guildford*: college of law publishing. 22

43 The investigation of Robert Culley whose body was exhumed and after investigation revealed that his wife, having takens 296,000 from an insurance company policy while the husband was on the sick bed, gave the husband rat poison consisting of thallium salt.

Evidence Act, 2011

The provisions of Section 31 of the Act appears dicey considering the fact that where a confessional statement is being obtained using the methods stated therein, it does not make an otherwise relevant confessional statement irrelevant. Such methods include promise of secrecy, deception and the suspect being drunk or not warned that he was not bound to make such statement and that evidence of it may not be given. Section 31 is in tandem with Section 14(a) & (b) of the Evidence Act, giving the court the discretion to exclude improperly obtained evidence:

> unless the court is of the opinion that the desirability of admitting the evidence is outweighed by the undesirability of admitting evidence that has been obtained in the manner in which the evidence was obtained

Section 29 (2)(a) & (b) however makes inadmissible confession obtained by the oppression of persons who made it or if made in an unreliable circumstance. The statement can also be retracted[44] by the accused person on the ground that the suspect never wrote a statement at all which goes to the weight and evidential value of the statement.[45] In case of an objection to the confessional statement, the decision in *Okonkwo v. The State* describes some factors to be considered in a trial within trial. These are factors neither taken care of in the laws discussed above. Some of these are:

---

44 *Ogbu v. State* (2000) FWLR. (pt.147) 1102 @1124-5,11-27 C.A., where there is prejudice to confessions as well as retraction of statement at the trial court cannot act upon such evidence.

d. *Chibuike vs. State* (2011) 1 FWLR. PART 559, 1172 - 1176; *Shande vs. State* (2005) All FWLR, (PT.279) 1342, *Okaroh V. The State* (1990) ANLR 130 at 137; *Adedara v. The State* (2009) 2FWLR; PT.478, 5057 @5067

- The condition and duration of the custody of the accused.
- Whether or not the legal advice of counsel was available to the accused before he made the confession.
- Whether or not the confession was retracted as soon as possible.
- The time and the place where and when the confession was made.
- Whether or not officers breached the laws of custodial interrogation at the time of confession.
- The content of the statement with respect to the level of the accused person's literacy.
- Sentence pattern in the statement to determine whether it is consistent with coherent tale or disorganized responses to police questions during interrogation.

Admissibility of Confession

The rules of admissibility in respect of confession has been pronounced in plethora of cases. Statements made by an accused person under investigation where adjudged voluntarily represent proof that can be used as a necessary fact against him at trial. Confession evidence is therefore the best evidence that can be led against an accused person. If such statement has been duly proved and admitted, it may alone, in some cases, be sufficient to warrant conviction.[46]

Therefore, a confessional statement if obtained willingly is a powerful proof and considered the best probably because it proceeds from a person's mind burdened by guilt with a willingness to relieve the weight of guilt from the mind. Any force, coercion,

---

46 *Babalola v. State* (2017) LPELR-42565(CA)10

pledge or lure from the police officer vitiates the statement and makes it inadmissible.

Section 29 provides for the use of confessions during criminal trials, and conditions for its admissibility, trial within trial, definition of oppression and exception to the rule. By Section 29 (4) of the 2011 Act, [47]confession can bind other defendants implicated in the confessions. An oral version of a confession to a witness can also be relied on by the prosecution or court even if a confessional statement was tendered and rejected or expunged before writing the judgment. The pre - trial nature of confessions was recognized in *Arogundade v. State*[48] that a confession could be oral or written and in this case it was both oral and in writing. Does the expunging of the written confession render inadmissible the oral version of the confession of the appellant to PW5 who was not the person before whom the written confession was made? It was answered in the negative.

By the 2011 Act, a confession if voluntary will be admissible notwithstanding that at the time it was made it had no relationship with the charge as it is no longer the law that the confession need be related with the accused person. Section 31 further buttressed this point while a confessional statement does not have to proceed from persons in authority as long as no oppression is used .The confessional statement should be voluntary as even the word obtain could vitiate its voluntariness. The rule of admissibility is relevancy. Based on *Torti vs Ukpabi*[49]admissibility is based on relevance and not proper custody and once a confession is relevant, the next in line is to establish it veracity which is usually done within a mini trial.

---

47 Formerly Section 27 (3) of the repealed Act.

48 (2009) ALLFWLR (pt.469) 4095

49 1984 S C. p.19; LPLER- 3259 (SC) Paras. L.E.

Trial within Trial

A mini trial is usually conducted along in the course of a criminal trial, it is a trial commenced before the substantive trial and judgment. What usually causes a trial within trial is when there is an objection to the voluntariness of the written statement. There are plenty of decided cases on it, however, it is established law that when objection is raised to a confession on the ground that it was never made by the accused at all, it is to be decided upon by the court at the conclusive end of the case and that confession can be admitted when tendered by the prosecution. Where however it is objected to at trial that the accused did not make the statement voluntarily, the trial-within trial will be undergone to test its voluntariness or otherwise.[50] During the mini trial, salient points are noted such as:

(a) The recording officer who obtained the statement at the police station must be called upon to give evidence. In most cases, when the accused person is objecting that the statement was obtained under duress or coercion, the onus is on him to prove same, thus the accused person will be called first to give evidence. Thereinafter all other necessary witnesses including the prosecution witness will be called to give evidence. There are certain factors in the course of this trial which would either substantiate or mitigate the accused's proof of the involuntary nature of the statement acquired.

(b) Proof of physical abuse by way of evidence showing that the accused person was physically tortured, bruises or injuries to show torture with medical evidence to prove same.

---

50 *Nwachukwu v. State* (2001) LPELR. 6183 C.A. Pp.22-23

(c) Proof of isolation as at the extraction of the statement shows likelihood of recording the confession under duress.

The statement itself should be properly scrutinized for discrepancies, inconsistencies because a person undergoing torture would not have his/her brain faculty in correct simulation to be able to relate it in a logical manner. A trial within trial is a test of discretion of the judge because at that juncture, he cannot predetermine the outcome of the case. The judge must focus solely on the voluntary element of the statement and not the culpability of the accused person. At this point, the judge is not supposed to look at the veracity of the statement, but how the statement was obtained. If obtained under duress, intimidation or moderate force, the statement should be rejected but if obtained in all due course following all protocol, then the statement should be admitted in evidence. The truthfulness or otherwise of the statement will be admitted to test when the defendant is duly cross-examined on the statement after the mini trial.

If a confession is opposed to because the accused persons never made the confession, then the retracted confession will still be admitted in evidence, but at the end of the case, the probative importance of such a confession will be considered.

There is thus a difference between denying making a statement and statement allegedly made with coercion.[51] The decision in *Demo Oseni v. The State*[52]recommends further that the confessional statement is well examined to be certain that the accused person

51 *Egboghonome v. The state* (1993) 7NWLR (PT.306) 383.
52 (2012) 5 NWLR (PT.1293) 351.

commits the act. An objection to a voluntariness of a confession would make the judge sitting alone to hear evidence on the point which may be tendered, and then rule on its admissibility, before receiving the confession in evidence or otherwise.[53] In *Dawa v. The State*[54] the trial court conducted seven mini trials within the main trial.

In *Banjo v. State*,[55] objection raised to the voluntariness of the confessional statement on the grounds of torture was rejected after a trial-within-trial, dismissing the evidence of torture. The appellant story was that two police officers, Hausa and Asumo hung him with a hanger, beating him with canes, machete and rope urging him to confess to the crime to which he eventually capitulated. The cross-examination of appellant on the said pieces of evidence was weak. Appellant went ahead to testify in the trial-within-trial that he was in fetters both on the hands and on the leg while his hands was hooked with the handcuffs to the ceiling fan in the small room. The drums were removed from under his feet and he was hanged, beating with the stick, cutlass and wire so as to confess, brought down forcefully and hit his head on the wall. There was no cross-examination on the fetters, both on the hands and on the legs as at the time he made the statement. Appellant's cross-examination revealed that his head, left arm and left leg sustained wounds from supposed torture. In admitting the statement in evidence, the court below did not advert itself to the fetters and chains under which the appellant was subjected when the statement was made nor did the court below make any observation on the officers as witnesses to clear the accusation by appellant that they participated in torturing him to give the confessional statement. The above identified lapses were not revisited or redressed in the judgment. The admissibility in

53 *Obidiozo V. State* (1987) 4 NWLR (Pt. 67) 748, at 760 – 761.

54 (1980) NSCC 334

55 (2012) ALLFWLR. (Pt.609) 1175 C.A

evidence of the confessional statement was observed fraught with death wounds.

Section 27 (2) and 28& 29 of Evidence Act,[56] provides what may vitiate the willingness of a confession to include inducement, threat or promise in reference to the accused person's charge proceeding from an individual in power and adequate, in the court's view, to offer the accused individual reasonable grounds for assuming that he would achieve, benefit or prevent any temporary evil by doing so. Section 28 & 29 of the Evidence Act, 2011 has however removed these vitiating factors replacing it with oppression and unreliability based on some circumstances.

The trial within trial is a fact finding trial to find out whether the confession can be properly admitted as part of the evidence when it is tendered by the prosecution. There are plethora of judicial interpretations on mini trial, when it will be conducted and the procedure to be adopted by court in such a trial. In such cases, where the accused person alleged that he was forced in making the statement or induced. In *Iorver &Ors v. State*[57] it was held that it is designed to ensure the voluntariness of the confession. If the voluntariness of the confessional statement was not proved at the end of the trial, it would not be admissible and it would be ruled accordingly; therefore, a confessional statement discovered not to have been voluntary should be expunged from the record if it was accepted incorrectly. The judicial interpretation in respect of whether confessions obtained during interrogation is voluntary is therefore germane as it determines whether the costs expended by the government in obtaining confession is worth the effort in the first place.

Which witness should be called first in a mini trial between the prosecution and the defence has not really been established by the

57 (2013) LPELR 20783 (CA)

courts. Some judicial authorities are to the effect that it is improper and will vitiates the trial to call the accused person first. In *Emeka vs. The State,*[58] such infringement may not affect the case if the accused person suffered no injustice. The investigating police officer would give evidence on how he came into the case, what transpired before, during and after recording the statement and if the statement was countersigned by a superior officer as to its voluntariness.

In *State v. Madukolu,*[59] what is expected from a superior officer when an accused person is taken before him is to demonstrate that the accused person actually made the alleged confession with no inducement like promise or threats to fulfill a need to further ensure that the accused person made a voluntary confession. If an interpreter apart from the investigating police officer is used, it will also be recorded, the superior police officer would then sign the statement while the accused person signs or thumb print.

With the above, the case of the prosecution will be further reinforced in the trial with additional facts and materials with which the court will reach a fair conclusion. This is due to the fact that where a statement is contested and still admitted in evidence it is regarded as the strongest means of proof. There is therefore need to properly scrutinized it.

The police diary has also been suggested as being very crucial in the absence of a detailed record of interview as stated above, which has being described as being very helpful in a trial within trial proceedings as the maintenance of a case diary can assist in reducing conviction error which would eventually lead to quashing on appeal.[60] *Onojaet.al*[61] is of the view that the judicial dicta in Nigeria

58 (2001) NWLR (PT.734) 666 at 682

59 (1972) 2ECSLR (pt.2) 623.

60 *Mbang v. State* (2009) 18 NWLR (Pt. 1172), 140

61 Onoja, E.O. *et.al* 2013, Refocusing the rules on admissibility of confessions in Nigeria to its constitutional Roots *Nigeria Bar Journal* Vol. 8, No. 1, ISSN 0795-54m 187-224.199

is not consistent about the treatment of confessions that are not preceded by a caution. According to him confession evidence are also not regarded as inherently forcible the way it is in some developed jurisdiction. The length of interrogation, denial or the unavailability of legal advice have not really been the focus of judicial interpretation in Nigeria.

In considering the principle that determines the admissibility of a confession objected to on grounds of involuntariness during trial within trial, each cases must be treated according to facts. In *State vs. Olashehu Salawu*[62]the respondent was tortured and that landed him in the hospital for two months, he was later taken to Ilorin where he was tortured to make a confessional statement. The prosecution however failed to call the vital witnesses named by the accused person to counter his statements which was fatal to the prosecution case, the medical record from the hospital was also not tendered and there was nothing outside the statement to corroborate it, hence its admission into evidence by the trial court was held wrong. In the *State v. Madukolum*[63]it was held that the interest of justice demands that every rule in favour of the accused person be rightly followed as any violation could prejudice the chances of the confessional statement at trial.

The question whether a confession obtained through a question and answer session conducted by the police amounts to oppression was considered and reckon with as a mixed grill in *Namsoh vs. State,*[64]Kutigi, J.S.C. held that a procedure whereby written questions are put to the suspect while investigating police officer records the answers is clearly wrong. An accused person must be cautioned first after arrest and if he or she wishes to get his statement written, he may so do or the police investigating police officer may write it for him. Any other method cannot be regarded as free and

---

62 *Ibid.*
63 (1993) 5NWLR (pt. 282) 144 at 179
64 (2011) 12 SC. (Pt.1) 130 P. 148

voluntary being answers to questions picked and put to the accused by the police officer himself.

The decision in *State vs. Jimoh Salawu,* varies a little though the confessional statement was expunged being products of questions and answers. There was actually no specific questions asked by the investigating police officers to which the statement was the answer. It is not a rule of criminal procedure law or that of evidence law for statements recorded from questions asked by a police officer to automatically become involuntary and inadmissible in law. The questions in Namsoh's case were prepared and oppressive having wearied and affected the accused person's mind and thus rendered his ensuing statement involuntary.

The solution to this quagmire lies in the manner the confession was recorded. In other words, to determine if questions and answers methods were used, the court in a trial within trial will have to construe the wordings of the questions and how the answers were recorded. It is in this manner that the flow of the questions will reveal whether or not it was the product of such oppressive conduct. This procedure was followed by the Supreme Court in *John vs. State,* where it was argued that the confessions objected to in *Namsoh vs. State*, were answers to a question and answer sessions with the suspect and hence were involuntary and therefore inadmissible. The Supreme Court unanimously dismissed this argument, holding that from the way they were recorded, the confessional statements were not the products of question and answer sessions.

In another perspective on the same case, the learned JSC is of the view that from the manner in which the confessional statements were recorded, the flow of language does not show that they were products of questions and answers session conducted by the police.

A confession proven to have been obtained as a result of things said or done in circumstances prevailing that is likely to render it vitiated is inadmissible in criminal trial.

The phrase has given the trial judge wide discretion and thus, nothing should stop a trial court from admitting a confession which, in his own judgment, is vitiated, even if the ground on which he is basing his judgment is not provided in Section 29 (2)

d. of the Act, if given the circumstances at the time it was made, he finds that it will be unduly prejudicial to the defendant to have the confession admitted. The power of the judge to reject any such confession because of any factor not mentioned in Section 29 of the Evidence Act is limited by the provision of Section 31, which has removed from the list of vitiating factors certain well-known and common law founded factors.

Anti –Torture Act, 2017

The Anti- Torture Act, 2017 is rather more detailed in listing out what constituted torture than in the Evidence Act, 2011. By so doing the rights of all persons, including suspects, detainees and prisoners are respected at all times.[65] Acts of torture is defined by the Act as acts that brings pain or suffering, physically or mentally during the extraction of information or a confession from suspects. It does not however includes pain or suffering in compliance with lawful sanctions.

Section 2 of the law provides a comprehensive definition of torture. According to section 2 (a), (i)- (xiv) of the Act, torture includes physical torture which refers to such cruel, inhuman or degrading treatment which causes pain, exhaustion, disability or dysfunction of one or more parts of the body such as: systematic beatings, head banging, punching, kicking, striking with rifle butts,

65 Commencement section of the Act.

jumping on the stomach etc. Section 2 (b) (i)-(ix) categorized psychological torture as mental or psychological torture, which is understood as referring to such cruel, inhuman or degrading treatment calculated to affect or confuse the mind or undermine a person's dignity or morale. It includes confinement in solitary cells put up in public places, prolonged interrogation to deny normal length of sleep or rest. Any confessional statement obtained in this manner is inadmissible in evidence, torture is therefore prohibited and punishment is 25 years under the law. Section 7 of the law makes all officers involved in the line of authority towards the carrying out an act of torture culpable.

Section 3 of the law recognizes that there is no condition under which torture is permissible, no exceptional cases including a state of war, political instability or other public emergency. Right to complain by the person who was torture or by another to a competent authority is allowed under the Act with assistance from the National Human Rights Commission, NGOS and private persons.

I submit that save as a result of the Panel that has been set up by various State Government in respect of the End SARS protest of 2020, the National Human Right Commission may not be efficiently equipped to assist in filing such complaints. This is so because the National Human Rights Commission have been found wanting in the handling of similar petition of human rights abuse in time past.[66]

The law has also increased suspects rights during pre- trial interrogations by imposing obligations on the police to inform a person arrested, detained or under custodial investigation of his right to demand a physical and psychological examination by an independent and competent Doctor of his choice after his

---

66 Op. cit. p.32

interrogation. This right however needs to be defined in the law with more detailed provisions to ensure same as well as penalty for non-compliance.

The Anti- Torture Act, 2017 has imposed more obligations on the police than other Acts or laws considered in this work in the following manner:

- Torture is now criminalized.
- Officers who commits torture or witness it, superior officer who aids, abets, counsels or protects it and superior Military police officer or senior government official who issues an order to a lower ranking police personnel to torture a victim for whatever purpose is liable as a principal.
- Officer can no longer use a state of war, emergency powers or orders from above as justification for using torture to obtain information or extract confessional statement.
- A police officer is obligated to inform a person arrested, detained or under custodial investigation of his right to demand a physical and psychological examination by an independent and competent Doctor of his choice after interrogation.

The Judges Rules, 1964

Judges rules came into use since 1912.[67] RULE 1 Interrogation of any person by the police in order to discover whether an offence has been committed.

RULE 11& 111 prescribe the caution to be administered to suspects before interrogation in terms of time and place, before questioning began and ended with the person present.

---

67 RULE V concerns statements made where more than one person is charged with the same offence. RULE Vı states that every police officer must comply with the rules

RULE 1V regulates the taking of written statements from suspects after the caution recorded in full, signed by the suspect or if he refuses, by the interrogator.

The old rules probably originated in the advice given in 1908 by the then lord Chief Justice in answer to an inquiry by a Chief constable which was later revised to assist themselves and guide policemen as to what was and what was not acceptable practice when taking statements from suspects.[68] The rules exist as a means of guidance for obtaining voluntary statement[69] with guidelines that do not have the power of law but administrative directives and conducive to reasonable administration of justice. However, it is essential that the police observe them, because statements made by suspects that are contrary to the spirit of these guidelines may be dismissed as proof by the judges who preside at the court.[70] Commonwealth countries have traditionally followed the Judges Rules, Nigeria inclusive before the enactment of the ACJA 2015.It set out processes for police officers during interrogation the taking of statements so as to guarantee that the suspects' statements were voluntary.[71]The Rules requires the police to caution suspects and inform them of their right to remain silent and that their statements could be used against them in trial.[72]

Adesiyan D.O. gave the reason for the introduction of the Rules in Nigeria being as a result of police use of force to obtain statement

68 RULE V concerns statements made where more than one person is charged with the same offence. RULE V1 states that every police officer must comply with the rules

69 The Judges Rule gave increasing judicial willingness to accept confessions into evidence obtained through interrogation. *R v. May* (1952)36 Cr. App.R. 91 at p.93

70 Lawrence J. in *R. vs. Voisin* (1982) 1 K.B 531

71 RCCP 1981 noted that the "Judges' Rules, represented a first conscious effort within the pre- trial procedure to set out a considered balance between the need to protect the rights of the individual suspect and the need to give the police sufficient powers to carry out their task.

72 Agbedo F. 2009 *Rights of suspects and Accused persons under Nigerian Criminal law* Crown Law publishers, 176

from suspects during interrogation.[73]R. *vs. Anya Ugwoga*[74]made it applicable to Nigeria to succeed it must be generally shown that the voluntary nature of the statement was tampered with before the court can use its discretion.[75]For as long as the caution was administered and it does not affect the voluntariness of the statement, it will be regarded as voluntary.[76]*In Usman v. State,*[77]the contention was whether a statement made in Hausa as well as in English translation were inadmissible as it was not read over to the accused person at the time of his making it nor was same signed by him. The court rejected this claim and held that Judges Rules breaches do not make a document inadmissible. At best, such breaches could only influence the weight of the statement attached by the court and definitely not its admissibility. The Rules impose on the Police to administer to a person being questioned, cautions at two stages of his interrogation that is:

when there is reasonable grounds for establishing the commission of the offence when charged or being informed that he may be prosecuted for a crime.

It is observed that may be the Judges Rule would have been better with a better police, and other appellate authorities independent of the court and the Police, like the Human Rights court in Strasbourg under the English Act of 1998. Section 31 of the Evidence Act has further reduced the effect of the Judges Rules and the use of caution while obtaining confession. In that it makes a confession relevant even when a suspect is not cautioned, or where custodial rules are violated. Caution alone where properly administered should safeguard the right of a suspect including

73 Adesiyan, D.O. 1996 *An Accused Person's Rights in Nigeria Criminal Law*, Heinemann Educational Books Nigeria p.67

74 1943, WACA 73,

75 There is a need to prove that the rule was not used by an Investigating Police officer who would then need to prove caution.

76 *State v Edekere* (1981) 2NCR 335.

77 CA/K/1/C/2004.

rights to silence and presumption of innocence without any statutory limitation or whatsoever. Earlier, the application of the Judges Rules by the police has been commended as a desirable practice, but where same is not applied, it will not vitiate the confessional statement, being regarded as a mere rule of administrative procedure and not rule of law that is mandatory.[78]An example, bringing an accused person before a superior police officer where his statement is read out and he is asked to confirm or deny it has been held to be mere rule of administrative practice and will not vitiate the statement if same is not complied with. Where that is not done however, the court will view the confession with considerable suspicion.[79] It is observed that this aspect of the Judges Rules later referred to is as developed by the courts in Nigeria and was not part of the Judges Rules designed by the Judges of the Kings Bench in England.

In *Abubakar vs. The State,*[80] It was held that these are rules of administration used by the police for obtaining confessional statement of the suspected person. Failure to apply same does not render the Confessional statement inadmissible. There are other rules of administrative practice in Nigeria apart from the Judges Rules in respect of custody interrogation.[81]

Judges Rules operate in this manner, once a police officer has proof that would provide reasonable grounds to suspect that an individual has committed an offence, he shall caution that individual or cause him to be cautious before placing any question or other issues before him. Other questions will be asked concerning the offence with the suspect not obliged to say anything unless he wishes to do so as whatever he says can be put in writing and put

78 Fakayode E. O 1977.*The Nigerian criminal code companion,* Ethiope Publishing Corporation, Ibadan, 111.

79 *Nwigboke & others vs.The Queen* (1959) 4 F.S.C. 101p.102

80 *Abubakar v. The State* (1969) NSCC 6.

81 Criminal Procedure (Statement to Police officers) Rules 1963.

in evidence. Where an individual is charged with or notified of being prosecuted for an offense, he shall be warned as well that he is free to say anything but not compelled to as whatever he says may not only be written down but may be provided as proof during trial.

It is only in extraordinary cases that issues concerning the offence should be addressed to the accused after being charged or notified that he may be prosecuted. Where needed, such questions may be placed in order to minimize damage to the individual, or to clarify an ambiguity in a prior response or statement. The latter is addressed by caution warnings that there is no obligation for answering any questions, however where such questions are answered it will be taken down in writing and given in evidence.

The suspects or someone writing for the suspect should make all written statements after caution. If he is unable to write, the suspect signs or create his mark before beginning, showing that the statement is true and was freewill given and he can make corrections to it. The person making the statement if he can write should write and sign before writing that he has read the statement and he could correct, alter or add anything he wishes and that the statement was truly made of his own freewill. If the statement is written by a police officer for a suspect, when he finishes, he shall be requested to read it and make any corrections, modifications or additions that he wishes. After reading it, at the end of the statement, he shall be told to write or register or a certificate similar to the one a suspect would have written had he written the statement himself.

International Treaty

Section 12 (1) of the 1999 Constitution of the Federal Republic of Nigeria makes a treaty between the Federation and any other country unenforceable except enacted into law. In essence, every international instrument to which Nigeria desires to be bound with should be domesticated and made subordinate to the Constitution. The decision in *Abacha v. Fawehinmi,* confirmed this position with the African Charter, which is domesticated already.[82]

It is still however a subject of debate that once an international treaty is signed and ratified by a country, it should abide by its regulations and that no other law should be enacted which is inconsistent with the said obligation.[83]

Of all the international instrument dealing with torture to which Nigeria is a party, it is only the African Charter that has mechanisms for its implementation based on judicial precedents which are not specifically provided for in the Charter. Actions based on it can be initiated by Writ of Summons or by the Fundamental Rights (Enforcement Procedure) Rules 2009.[84]

Convention against Torture and Other Cruel, Inhuman or Degrading Treatment or Punishment, 1984

The Convention against Torture and Other Cruel, Inhuman or Degrading Treatment or Punishment also referred to as the Torture Convention was adopted by the General Assembly of the United Nations on 10 December 1984.[85] The Convention is currently ratified by 20 states including Nigeria after it came into force on the 26th of June 1987.[86]

The Commission on Human Rights was set up on the 8th of December 1977 by the General Assembly by way of resolution preceding its adoption to study the question of torture and any

82 *Abacha V Fawehinmi* (2001) CHR 20 at 42; *Ubani v. Director of State Security Services &anor,* (1999) 11 NWLR 129

83 *Chief J.E Oshevire V British Caledonian Airways Limited,* (1990) 7 NWLR (Pt.163) p.507 at pp.519-520:

84 In *Abacha V Fawehinmi,* (2001) WRN 29 ,274

85 Resolution 39/47

86 Nigeria signed the convention on the 28th of July, 1988 but ratified the convention on the 28thof June, 2001

necessary steps for guaranteeing its effective compliance.[87] It began working on the subject at its session in February/March 1978. Discussions by the different working groups centered mainly on issues like the definition of torture; universal jurisdiction for torture within and outside the territory of the offender's member state nationality such as found in conventions against hijacking of aircraft and other terrorist acts and implementation for the purpose of effectiveness which later resulted into the setting up of the Committee against Torture.[88]

The committee was saddled with many tasks as stated in Articles 17, 19, 20, 21,22 and 28, of the Convention. Torture is regarded as a criminal offence within the legal system of state members while obligations as to implementations are found in Articles 2, 3,4,6,7,12, 13, and 14 of the convention. The Committee against Torture holds two annual sessions to examine reports from States parties orally in the presence of one or more representatives of the State concerned. Each State whose report is to be examined at a session is informed in advance of the main questions the Committee wishes to be discussed and the Committee then adopts its conclusions and recommendations. The Committee may also adopt general comments on specific provisions of the Convention or issues related to their implementation.

An Optional Protocol to the Torture Convention was later adopted by the General Assembly of the United Nations on 18 December 2002[89] and entered into force on the 22nd of June 2006. It establishes a system of regular visits by international and national bodies to places of detention in order to prevent torture and other cruel, inhuman or degrading treatment or punishment. A

87 Resolution 32/62.

88 Article 17 of the Torture Convention, 1984

89 resolution 57/199

Subcommittee on Prevention of Torture was also established to visit, assist and perform similar function at the national levels.

The Right of Suspects under the Criminal Procedure Code

In the North, the Criminal Procedure Code applies and by virtue of Section 38 of the law,[90] a suspect has the right to be informed of the cause of the arrest except when the person arrested is in the actual course of committing a crime, or is pursued immediately after committing a crime or escaping from lawful custody. By Section 39 (1) of the law, any person save a police officer or a Justice of the peace shall without unnecessary delay take the person arrested to the nearest police station or hand him over to a police officer. It is observed that rights of the accused person are provided for but that of suspects are sparsely captured by that law at the pretrial stages including while obtaining their statements.

Interpreter: The language of the court is English, where however evidence is given in a language different from what the accused person understands in court, there arises a need to interpret it to him in a language understood by him.[91] An interpreter must be provided for an accused person for better comprehension of the charge against him because he is entitled to it.

---

90 The Administration and Criminal Justice Act, 2015 has not repealed this law.

91 Section 241 Criminal Procedure Code

8

THE ENGLISH MODEL OF LEGAL FRAMEWORK REGULATING CONFESSIONS

Police and Criminal Evidence Act, 1984 (PACE) (As Amended)

PACE provides for the powers of police officers in England and Wales in combatting crimes, it is supported by the Codes for the implementation of those powers[1] and in accordance with Part VI of PACE.[2] Section 66 makes provision for the use of police powers including the associated rights and safeguards for Suspects and the public in England and Wales. The PACE is a strictly controlled legislative scheme for criminal investigation so as to check Police discretion and make it constitutional and conforming to case laws.[3] The procedure for recording confessional statement under PACE is more elaborate than ACJA and gives guidance to the exercise of powers of the police on processes and suitable treatment of suspects and defending the rights of members of the public. The PACE emerged from the need to put together provisions that were piecemeal and haphazard with powers of arrest included in 70 different statutes. Audio recording and visual recording with sounds of interviews are provided for under section 60 (1) of the law.

Devices are specified and authorized for implementation purposes. An example is a body worn Video (BWV) which is a suitably compliant authorized recording device. Written record is allowed

---

1 Police and Criminal Evidence Act, 1984 (as amended)

2 ibid.

3 Leigh,l. H. ,1985. *Police powers in England and Wales*. London, Butterworths, p.31

without delay where it is certified that suitable device is not accessible. Visual recording is made simultaneous with audio recording in accordance with Code E. Recently, live link was introduced such that there can be an interview between sergeants and detainee from different stations; between officers outside the police station in whose custody the suspect is; a suspect can see, hear and have conversations with the officers in the other station, etc. Other officers that can engage in live link include; interview officers, review officers, authorizing officers etc. Section 67 (4) of PACE requires the home Secretary, if he/she wishes to review codes of Practice, have statutory consultation[4]with certain people which is a critical element in the development of the PACE Codes.[5]

PACE [6] is stringent with criminal liability for violations of the Act and the Code during searches, arrests, detention and the interview of a suspect and may lead to exclusion of evidence in court. The focus here is on rights of suspects during extraction of confessional statements hence, the emphasis is on the Codes for interviews and treatment of suspects.[7]It is applicable to police officers and those that conduct criminal investigation including, Customs, and the military as far as practical and relevant.[8]

4 The last consultation was from the 24thof October to the 6thof December, 2018. It introduces new definition of Vulnerable. Suspects are to be informed of all the rights, entitlements and safeguards that will apply, to be asked to give consent to the interview and to be given a notice to explain the matters.

5 Revised Codes C, H, E and F laid before Parliament 21stof May ,2018

6 Equivalent provision is made for Northern Ireland by the Police and Criminal Evidence (Northern Ireland) Order 1989 (SI 1989/1341). The equivalent in Scots Law is the Criminal Procedure (Scotland) Act 1995.

7 Other areas in which the police powers are given powers include powers to search an individual or premises, including their powers to gain entry into those premises and the handling of exhibits seized from those searches. Specific legislation as to more wide-ranging conduct of a criminal investigation is contained within the Criminal Procedures and

8 Codes must be available at all Police station

Section 82(1) of PACE as amended defines a confession as any statement wholly or partly adverse to the person who made it, whether made to a person in authority or not whether made in words or otherwise. Section 76 of the law deals with the challenges to the admissibility of confessions in criminal trials and directs the tribunal to exclude confession evidence obtained by oppression or in circumstances which were likely to render the confession unreliable. Facts discovered as a consequence of the confession or the manner in which the defendant speaks, writes or expresses himself may be adduced under Section 76 (4) of the law. Section78 of the law gives the court the discretion to exclude evidence otherwise admissible against a defendant on the grounds that it would be unfair to adduce it, while Section 66 and 67 are intended to enable the court to correct the unfairness arising from criminal proceedings.

Statements made by a suspect that do not contain admissions are not liable to exclusion in accordance with section 76.[9]This is because object made against a defendant's statement during the trial on the grounds that they are incorrect or incompatible do not imply that the statements are confessed for the reasons of section 76.[10]

Despite its various provisions, acceptance was extremely debatable at its onset. Its reviews also came up for debates over the extensive powers given to the police. Di Birch[11] describes confessions admitted in evidence under the Act as first class because of quality control measures and the 3 stringent tests that the confession(s) are subjected to during trial which must be satisfied before its admissibility. According to him section 76(1) and Section 76 (2) a and b gives the standard of an admissible confession in evidence. That is, if the confession was or may have been obtained by

9 *R. vs. Sat. Bhambra* 1989 88 CR APP 55

10 Section 82 (1) of PACE; *R v. Park* 99 Cr. App R.270.

11 Birch D. 1989 The PACE Hots Up: Confessions and confusions under the 1984 Act. *The Criminal. L.R.*P.96

oppression of the person who made it; or obtained in consequence of anything said or done which was likely, in the circumstances existing at the time to render unreliable any confession which might be made by him in consequence thereof.

The existence of any of the grounds above at the presentation or use of a confession evidence in court vitiates the confession which shall not be made use of except in so far as the prosecution proves to the court beyond reasonable doubt that the confession notwithstanding (which may be true) was not obtained as aforesaid. Defence can use any of the grounds to object to the admissibility of a statement and where the veracity cannot be proved, the confession shall not be admissible.

Be that as it may, the prosecution before sailing through tendering of a confessional statement may have to pass through another hurdle in Section 78 of checking that the evidence obtained does not have an adverse effect on the fairness of the proceedings for which the court would not admit it.

Any evidence that affects the fairness of the proceedings in court will be excluded. The section in conjunction with section 76 (1) and (2) offers a double protection to the quality of confessions to suspects whose pretrial rights were breached or violated and for which objection cannot be raised under section 76 2(a) and (b).

Section 76 (2) (a) and (b) foistered the burden of proof on the prosecution, while section 78 embodies a discretionary power to be exercised on the part of the judge. The fairness discretion calls attention to any inappropriateness in the method of obtaining the evidence. Section 82(3) empowers the court to exclude evidence whether by preventing questions from being put to the suspect indiscriminately or otherwise at its discretion and this is without prejudice to other provisions in the Act. This section extends to all types of evidence upon which the prosecutor may seek to rely including confessional evidence. The section also preserves the common law discretion to exclude evidence.

Section 82 (3) was interpreted in *Mason,*[12]wherein a confession was obtained from the accused person whose solicitors deliberately misinformed him about the importance of the evidence in the possession of the police. The confession was excluded under section 78 because of the misconduct. Sections 76 and 78 has been argued to be limited to the initial part of a criminal trial and before a confessional statement is put in evidence because both have clauses in it to that effect. Also, according to Section 78 the confessional evidence may be refused from being given in evidence. The common law discretions do not need to be invoked in cases where an issue is taken before the evidence is given.[13]

Section 76 of the PACE and section 29 of the Evidence Act, 2011 represents a break with past traditions under which the key factor that can vitiate the admissibility of a confessional statement was based on inducement. Under that regime, anything said or done to cause the potentially unreliable confession and by whom as well, whether no impropriety occurred does not matter. In *Harney,*[14] the fact that the suspect heard her lover confess to murder was held sufficient to induce the woman being of low intelligence to give false confession to protect her lover. Her statement was excluded under Section 76 (2) (b). Breaches of rules whether contained in the PACE or the Codes may supply evidence of unreliability.

The rule of exclusion if based on oppression brings the focus on the evidence and erring officer. This is because where oppression is found, automatic exclusion to the misconduct follows. Torture, inhuman or degrading treatment, and the use of threat or violence,

---

12 (1987) 3 ALLER. 481

13 Ibid. p.99

14 (1988) Crim. L.R 241

whether it amounts to torture or not comes within the purview of oppression in Section 78(8) of PACE. The question of what includes came up in *FULLING,*[15] *where* D had been questioned about an insurance fraud in which she and her boyfriend were alleged to have taken part. She made no disclosure until she claimed one of her interrogators adopted the unsporting method of deceit of telling her that her boyfriend has a lover who was detained in a cell close to hers. She was so distressed that she confessed in order to escape from the police station. The common law definition of oppression was artificially wide. Hence, the question to be asked is whether cases of oppression have potential for unreliability? The tactic used to extract a confession from *Fulling* was an example of such a case.

Oppression was also described as an exercise of power in a heavy, severe or wrongful manner, unjust or cruel treatment of subjects, inferiors and the imposition of unreasonable or unjust burdens.[16] Not having access to a legal practitioner's advice is regarded as oppressive. It has been argued that there cannot be oppression without impropriety but the converse does not follow. In *Samuel,*[17] D's lack of access to a legal practitioner though an impropriety is regarded as oppression because the denial of access was to break down the right to silence.

Where the admissibility of confessional evidence is questioned in accordance with section 76 of the prosecution, it must be established without reasonable doubt that the confession was not actually produced as a consequence of oppression or in conditions that were likely to make it unreliable. What was likely in the circumstances existing at the time, was interpreted in *R. vs. Moses*[18] as that which owes its origin directly to that which was said or

15 (1987) 2ALL E.R 65.
16 Ibid p.69
17 (1988) 2 ALL E.R. 135,
18 (1990) 91 CR, APP.R 37

done[19] while oppression includes torture, inhuman or degrading treatment and the use of threat or violence.[20] This definition is similar to the one provided in article 3 of the European Convention on Human Rights. Oppression in the convention was defined as something which tend to sap and has sapped the freewill which exist before the confession.[21]An example is the using of chains on the defendant's leg.

It has also been held that overly prolonged and excessive use of force during police interrogation constitutes threat or oppression, which would render inadmissible any confession obtained as a result. In *Burnt vs. Public Prosecutor*[22] the Privy Council held that making suspects to wear hoods and manacles during interrogations amounted to oppression and makes the alleged confessional statements unacceptable.

On the other hand, it is permissible for an investigating police officer or other interrogators to use raised and harsh language when the person interrogated is tough and any confession obtained from him will not be rendered inadmissible thereby. But this alone will not render admissible a confession obtained after several denials, but which was induced by heavy and oppressive verbal bullying of the suspect by police officers, even though counsel to suspect was around during the interrogation but chose rather to remain silent.

In R. vs Smith[23] a private soldier who was amongst other soldiers accused of certain offences, was taken before his Regimental Sergeant-Major, who had threatened that the defendant and other soldiers would be stood on the parade ground until the perpetrator of the crime had confessed to it. This made the defendant repeated

19 *Re Pronx Sub Nom R vs. Bow Street Magistrates court* (2001) ALLER 57

20 Section 29 (5) of the Evidence Act 2011.

21 *R vs. Priestly* (1967) 5 Cr, Appeal R.12; *R vs. Prager* (1972) 56 Cr App. R 151

22 (1995) 2 AC 597

23 (1969) 2 Q.B 35

the confession after he was cautioned and interrogated by another soldier directed to interrogate him, the first confession was held not free and inadmissible because it put the appellant in difficulty, the second one was admissible because the effect of any original inducement or threat under which the first statement was made had been dissipated.

The word oppression was defined in *R. vs. Fulling* as an exercise of authority or power in a burdensome, harsh, or wrongful manner; unjust or cruel treatment of subjects, inferiors etc. and the imposition of unreasonable or unjust burdens, while in *R. vs. Parker*[24], the word wrongful was defined as burdensome, harsh and unjust or cruel treatment.

The degree of prolonged questioning by the police or interrogators is always to be weighed against the defendant's intelligence and level of education. Earlier before PACE, it was lawful to conduct prolonged, rigorous interrogations of experienced, professional or other sophisticated suspects, while deploying softer interrogation tactics on younger or weaker suspects, in such cases as earlier held that such rigorous interrogation did not amount to oppression.

In *R. vs. Priestly,* Sachs, J.,[25] held that oppression has different meaning for different cases, including length of time for questioning, intervening periods between questioning, refreshment or not and character of the statement. What may be oppressive as regards a child, an invalid or an old man or somebody inexperienced in the ways of this world may be the opposite for a suspect who is already toughened on the street.

Individual differences notwithstanding, a confession obtained from any suspect as a product of repetitive and harsh verbal bullying and hectoring was inadmissible on the ground that it was obtained

---

24 (1995) Crim. L.R 233

25 (1967) 51 C.R. App R. 1

under an oppressive atmosphere; the presence of the suspect's counsel notwithstanding and counsel not objecting to the manner of interrogation. However, where the interrogators merely occasionally raised their voices and asked aggressive questions, this was held not to amount to oppression.

In the New Zealand case of *Italian Holdings (Properties) Ltd. vs. Lonsdale Holdings (Auckland) Ltd.*[26], Vautier, J., held that oppressive conduct means some real detriment or hardship. Also, in *Horvath vs.* R.,[27] a 17-year-old boy was mesmerized before he made the purported confession and he was shown to be under emotional disintegration during questioning. There was prolonged questioning under those conditions, the confession was not admitted in evidence as the psychiatrist during trial said the defendant was under an atmosphere of oppression that gave him a sense of being threatened. The statement was excluded based on the type of techniques, age of the accused, the circumstances, the hours of the morning when the questioning was done and the length of the interrogation in an atmosphere of oppression that is threatening.

The involuntariness of the statement was affirmed on appeal based on the fact that the 17 years old was of most unstable character, a sociopath with a make believe that he is the owner of three vehicles and a manager of a department of a large company and having told another person of his age that he was so anxious to have a car and could kill his mom and get the money from her. He was held to be in a state of complete emotional disintegration.

Oppression also cropped up in R *vs. Fulling,*[28]and was held would likely involve some misconduct on the part of the interrogator, while unreliable Confession include confessions obtained by inducement, a bail promise or acquittal/ discharge promise, hostile

26 (1984) 2 NZLR 1at 15
27 (1979) 7C.R. 3d Supreme Court of Canada.
28 *R vs. Fulling,* (1987) 2ALL E.R 65

and aggressive interrogation, failure to correctly record what has been said, lack of caution, unavailability of responsible adult to act where necessary and noncompliance with PACE codes. Others includes in relation to the detention of the accused like, inadequate rest before an interview and defense solicitor or appropriate adult not behaving correctly, such as making interjections harmful to the defendant during an interview.

In *R vs. Moss,*[29] a confession made by a defendant who was shown to be of low intelligence, and who was denied access to legal advice, was inadmissible based on the fact that it is not reliable. Confession must owe its origin directly to that which was said or done for it to be reliable. In *Re Proulx, sub norm R. vs. Bow Street Magistrates Court,*[30] the Canadian police had suspected P, who was living in England, of having committed a murder in Canada. In order to obtain evidence, they launched an undercover operation in England, with the cooperation of the local police. P made statements to the Canadian police officer admitting to the murder during undercover. At the trial for P's extradition, the Stipendiary Magistrate found that those confessions is in compliance with Section 9(8) (a) of the Extradition Act 1989, and ordered P's commitment to detention pending the decision of the Secretary of State to return him to Canada. P applied for habeas corpus and judicial review, contending that the confessions ought to have been excluded under Section 76(2) (b) of PACE as being obtained in subsequence of something said or done which in the circumstance have rendered the confession unreliable. In the alternative, the confession would be excluded under Section 78c of the 1984 Act, which gave the court discretion to reject evidence if, taking into account all the circumstances in which the evidence was acquired, its admission would have such an adverse effect on

29 (1990) 91 Cr. App. R. 371
30 (2001) 1All ER 57

the fairness of the proceedings that the court should not admit it. The meaning of the term any confession in section 76(2)(b) of the PACE Act, 1984, was to be understood as meaning any such or such a confession made by a defendant which is the relevant confession and not an entirely different confession. In addition, it is unreliable where the confession was recorded from the consequence of things said or done that were likely in the circumstances to render it so. Admissibility would be considered by a magistrate based on:

(a) What was said or done,

(b)The circumstances existing at the time of the confession,

Section 77 of that law also provides additional measures for those who are mentally handicapped, who are in a state of arrested or incomplete development of mind which includes significant impairment of intelligence and social functioning.

Under PACE, where it appears that a confession evidence is likely to be challenged on the grounds of admissibility, steps could be taken to obtain additional evidence to cover the circumstances in which it was made.[31] Statement from the custody record and a statement from a forensic physician who examined the suspect during the relevant period may be useful to rebut any allegation that the suspect was abused by officers. A significant breach of the law will lead to exclusion in court, not frivolities; and a challenge for admissibility under this Act is not on truthfulness but voluntariness.[32]

Challenges on section 76 takes place in the Crown or the Magistrate court by the prosecutors or on the courts volition in a Voire Dire (mini trial). Defendant may call a witness to support or not, while

---

31 In Nigeria, files could be returned to the Police only at the point of rendering a legal advice where there is a need for additional facts.

32 *R. vs. Davis1 990Crim. Law Review.* 860

court is not concerned with truthfulness of the confessions.[33] Challenges under section 78 do not usually involve a trial within trial, except the defence challenged admissibility under both S.76 & 78 of the law.

In respect of the Questioning Code and its revision, Wolchover et al,[34] discussed the practical impact of the changes made with suggestions for further impact of informing suspect of the right to a solicitor which is not available under the old code on first suspicion /arrest in the field, but available for formal detention at the police station. According to him, the old code contains little to guarantee the right to consult a lawyer, although there is notification of free legal advice. In the past, detainees declined the advice on the grounds that they could not afford it. By the new Code, every police station charging area must display the instruction toward right to counsel and it is now an ongoing right that can be exercised at any stage during the custody period.

Authenticating real waiver of legal advice is important to avoid false claim by the police of waiver of legal advice while a refusal to sign be interpreted as wanting advice.[35] A research carried out by Birmingham University and published by the lords Chancellor's department confirmed the worst fears about abuse which had been circulating amongst practitioners for years.[36] In particular, the researchers noted a resort to the ploy of exploiting detainees' disoriented state by rushing them through the drill so briskly that they clearly had little opportunity to absorb what was being put across. This right to be reminded of a right to a solicitor before interview continues prior to the commencement or

33 Section 76 (2) & 3

34 Wolchover D. et.al 1991; The Questioning Code Revamped,*The Crim. L Review*,232 249.234

35 This provision is not in the Administration of Criminal Justice Act, 2015

36 Sanders A. et.al 1989; Advice and Assistance at Police stations and the 24 hour Duty solicitor scheme,*Crim.l. Review* 495-509

recommencement of any interview at the police station.[37] It was also suggested that the time of notification, signed waiver or agreement should be recorded prior interview. There is an improved structure for notifications of right based on the amended Code and circulars.

When PACE was being legislated, the Government had recognized the principle that there is little purpose in providing a right to a suspect if awareness of that right is to be left to chance. I think that this reality is being left to chance under the ACJA. For example, the Act, though provided for notification of counsel, the understanding of the right, its affordability and availability of the services is not certain. What if lawyers from the Legal Aid Council are not available or there is delay in the coming of a lawyer? What if there is a waiver? Who records it? And if the suspects now opt again for a legal representatives? What will happen in such cases? These are questions to be answered.[38]

Safeguards must be administered early at certain points in the process between the officer and the suspects arrested before it becomes a full blown interrogation. On the street interview is new and developing with minimal protection which can give room to abuse, impropriety from officers and fabrication of witnesses. Fenwick[39] is of the view that the protection offered a suspect interview on the street is too minimal and could lead to impropriety and abuse on the part of the officers and fabrication of confessions.

37 Paras 112, 1991 revised Code.

38 The Administrative Directions on interrogation and the taking of statements published in conjunction with the 1964 Judges Rules

39 Fenwick H.1993, Confessions, Recording rules and miscarriages of justice, a mistaken emphasis,*Crim. L. R.* 174-183.

Under PACE, some improprieties falls short of oppression but still led to the exclusion of the statement such as is found in the case of *Absalom.*[40] D, was arrested on suspicion of threatening behavior. While the custody officer recollected that he was released earlier on bail for drug crimes, he was requested to bring out the contents of his pocket to which he obliged. Acting on what must have been inspiration, the officer added that he should now put the drugs on the table and much to his astonishment, D produced a quantity of cannabis resin after some questioning. D was not told of his right to legal advice and no contemporaneous record was made of the interview. On appeal, the court decided that there was a breach of the codes. Link was established between the breaches and the evidence obtained while the evidence was excluded at trial.

Examples of gamut of illegality and impropriety falling short of oppression includes:

(1) Oppressive conduct which does not fall under section 76, but linked to the obtaining of evidence e.g., where a defendant was beaten up after confession.

(2) Deliberate breach of various rights involved in the interrogation process or willful impropriety casually linked to obtaining the evidence but fall short of the wickedness required for oppression. An example is the inaccessibility to legal advice which can encourage the suspect to talk without guidance during questioning.

(3) Negligent cases or blameless infringement of rights or other conduct which turns out to be harmful or misleading but which is indulged in innocently.

---

40 (1988) CRIM L.R. 748

To consider a confessional evidence for exclusion under section 78, the court would consider the right violated, extent of any impropriety involved, the rate of public interest denouncing the nature of the offence and the interest of justice. Impropriety is a reprehensible conduct on the part of the police and in *Mason's*[41]Watking L.J. stated that the deceit practiced upon the appellant's solicitor is actually reprehensible and the judge could use its discretion to exclude the confession obtained thereby.

Disciplinary motivation does not arise in the application of section 78 as there should be a causal link between the breach and the confession. In cases like *Alladice, Hughes*[42] and *Osman Samuel,*[43] there is a common view that bad faith provides an almost automatic ticket to exclusion. All the cases are concerned with access to legal advice. In *Doolan,*[44] breaches of the code in relations to cautioning and interview were regarded as likely in the circumstances existing at the time to render the evidence unreliable. It is so for a mentally or handicapped defendant. Anything said or done will not include question properly but conditions such as the presence of an independent adult required by the codes of practice.[45]

Codes of Practice

Code A relates with the exercise of police officers to search a person or a vehicle without first making an arrest, it was later amended on 1st of January, 2009 to the extent that the police officer will need to account for the recording procedures of not lengthy stop or encounter. They are required to only record a subject and to issue them with a receipt.

41 (1987) 3 ALLER 481
42 1988 Crim.LR 545,
43 (1988) 2 ALLER 13
44 (1988) Crim L.R. 747
45 Code C, 13 and Annex.

Code B deals with police powers to search premises, seize and retain property found on premises and persons.

Code C provides the requirement for the detention, treatment and questioning of people in police custody by police officers replacing the Judges' Rule in England and Wales.[46]

PACE[47] is supplemented by 5 Codes of Practices, including Codes C and E. Section 67 (11) PACE made the Codes applicable to evidence during proceedings in court and where relevant, it shall be taken into account in determining that question. Code C is specifically applicable to appropriateness of the suspects to be interviewed with guidance for arrest, custody handling and questioning of persons. [48]

By paragraph 6 of Code C, detained persons must be informed of their rights to consult a solicitor privately, whether by individual, contact in writing or by telephone. The availability of free independent advice, the right to have someone informed about their arrest, the right to consult the codes of practice with a poster showing the rights to be displayed in the police station's charging region is very crucial. A suspect may not be interviewed without

---

46 Code C; detainees must be informed that they may at any time consult and communicate privately with a solicitor whether in person, in writing or by telephone for free advice. Code C 2014; requirements for detention treatment and questioning of suspect not related to terrorism in police custody by police officers include the requirement to explain a person 's rights while detained.

47 A law that modernizes, rationalizes the law governing police powers and to reform aspect of the law relating to criminal evidence, heralded tape recording of interview in police stations and the police to keep records of their dealings with suspects at all stages.

48 Revision of Codes within the Pace Act 1984 was laid by Damia Green on 21st of October 2013 in the house of commons and in the House of Lords by Lord Taylor of Holbeach; Code C 2014, Requirement for detention, treatment and questioning of suspect not related to terrorism in police custody by police officers include the requirement to explain a person's rights while detained; Code D,2011. Keeping of accurate records and reliable criminal records; Code E,2016 Audio recording of interview with suspects in the police station; Code F 2016, Visual recording interviews; Code H. Home officers 2003, p. 47. Amended 11/5/2012; 1/2/2008; 15/7/2012;21/10/ 2013;2016;2017

seeking legal advice unless there is a limitation on drawing adverse inferences. Code C also provides for appropriately qualified independent persons and extends to impediments to speech.

Suspects arrested in a police station must be notified of their legal rights in any 24hr period and an uninterrupted rest period of not less than 8 hours. Suspects mentally incapacitated or young is entitled to a responsible adult recognized as an appropriate adult whose role is to advise and communicate further and guarantee that the interview is well conducted. All interviews must be registered electronically in the UK so as to instill trust in its reliability, impartiality and drives to guarantee its integrity, must be carried out publicly.

Interview records is strictly supervised by authorized individuals for accuracy purpose including investigating officers and prosecutors, including copying to removable media only. Code C also takes care of interview records safety, statements are to be stored on non-removable storage systems in read-only format; for instance, hard disk.

It should be noted that the investigative interview in the United Kingdom is less confrontational in contrast to the Reid technique in the United States, *Bull* et al. noted in their research that tactics of maximization and minimization based on confrontations are rarely used in England.

Code D is about the main methods used by the police to identify people in connection with the investigation of offences and the keeping of accurate and reliable criminal records.[49]**Code E** deals with the tape recording of interviews with suspects in the police station.[50]**Code F** deals with the visual recording with sound of interviews with suspects. [51] **Code G** came up on 1st of January, 2006which deals with statutory powers of arrest.

49 Code D 2011: keeping of accurate record and reliable criminal record

50 Code E 2016, Audio recording of interview with suspects in the police station

51 Code F 2016, Visual recording of interviews.

On 24 July 2006, a further code H came into force dealing with the detention of[52] terrorism suspect. Revision to Code C and H transfer the legal obligations in the European Union Directive[53] on the right to interpretation and translation in criminal proceedings into UK domestic legislation. The amendments made room for suspects to be assisted in communications and to understand why they are detained, the nature of the charge brought against them and having access to an interpreter and written translations of documents as necessary.

Amendments to Code E and F is for the conduct and recording of voluntary interviews of suspects who are not under arrest. A sergeant is responsible for the interviews and for giving the authority for them not be audio recorded. They also connect a number of cross references to the code of practice for the video recording of interviews of terrorist detainers. There is also an amendment concerning the security of master interview recordings in order to ensure consistency between codes C and F and the new terrorism code.

Operations under PACE, 1984 & Codes: The various operations are as follows:

(a) Attached Circulars

The PACE home office circulars 76/1988 supplies guidance on tape recording in respect of training of officers on investigative interviewing skills and preparation of the records of tape for recorded interview.[54]

52 Code H 2016,

53 2010/04/EU

54 HOC 39/1991

(b) Interviews under Caution commonly known in HSE as PACE interview

Interviews under Code C also known as HSE is an interview carried out with caution and audio –recording subject to the limited exceptions in PACE Code E. A suspect not under arrest can be interviewed at a certain place for example at an HSE office apart from a police station. Administration of caution is the starting point, after that comes the putting of the significant statement or silence to the suspect, whether or not it was earlier stated before a first interview or a subsequent one, accepted or refused for the purpose of denying or confirming it and whether the suspect wants to add anything.

(c) Oppressive Interview Techniques

Use of oppression to obtain answers is disallowed under HSE, as it could lead to the exclusion of the evidence. Final outcomes of questioning is not disclosed to suspect, whether the suspect answers the questions put to him or not or giving as an answer to direct question from the suspect.

Suspect must not be left unattended during an interview, while recorder should still be on during short breaks and in the presence of all parties, except at breaks during the interview at which time it is expected that the audio recording should stop. Breaks must be announced before it is taken while the time and reasons for switching off the recorder must be recorded. Where there is a break and suspect leave the room, the tape or CD should be ejected from the recorder and sealed. The interview will continue with a new tape or CD through the earlier procedure.

After resumption from break, continuation of interview should be announced and recorded and the reason why the break was taken will be repeated with the time the session is starting again.

Suspect should be reminded of their caution or the caution could be re-administered.

(d) Ending the Interview

The interview or further interview of suspects ceases when:

a. As soon as all necessary and relevant questions about the offence has been exhausted, all ambiguities cleared and all answers given with accuracy and reliability, the interview must cease.

b. Account have been taken of any other available evidence; and

c. There is reasonable believe and sufficient evidence to provide a prospect of conviction.

(e) Audio Recorded interview under caution

Audio recording an interview under caution ensures accuracy and is the best way to ensure evidence is taken under an atmosphere of reduced coercion. Code E on the revised Code of Practice on audio recording interviews with suspects is considered along with Code C on the questioning and treatment of persons. The court may exclude evidence of the interview if a relevant provision of the code particularly C& D is not followed.

(f) Equipment for Recording

Code E provides for recording using any removable, physical audio recording medium that can be played and copied on a secure digital network. In HSE, interviews under caution are recorded on tape or CD. The Guidance on tape requires that every office has an equipment for recording and matters including how to prepare for the interview and how to operate the machine be spelled out. Equipment includes record- only recorder that can record two or three tapes or CDs at a time with time display to show when it elapsed like every 10 seconds. Blank CDs or tape must be sealed, after which a recording notice would be given to the suspect whose interview was recorded.

(g) Recording Media

At the interview and during the production of the master recording, tapes or CDs are newly opened in the presence of the suspect from its sealed state and loaded into the machine, after the interview, it will be sealed in the presence of the suspect to be opened in court being the master recording. The second copy and third copy is the working copy and suspect's copy, the latter may be given to the suspect if requested. Each office have arrangements for tape and CD security.

If during an interview, the recorder indicates the media only have a short time left, the suspect will be informed that the recording is ending and round off that part of the interview. The next step of tapes/CDs are then unwrapped and load into the machine in the presence of the suspect.

(h) Recording the Interview

Recording of interview starts with introduction of the recorder, his/ hername and post, the place of interview, the date and time, voices of all other persons present in the room are also recorded as they get introduced. The suspect is also required to give his or her names in full address, date of birth and, where the suspect is an individual, National Insurance Number.[55]

Suspect are informed of the recording processes and what will happen at the end of the interview. Interviews are done under caution and suspect must be told that they are not under arrest and are free to leave. Other rights of suspect here include the right to legal advice, if there is no solicitor present during the procedure.

---

55 These details will be required if legal proceedings are subsequently initiated.

A person nominated by a company may speak on behalf of a company, if given the power to do so, the person only needs to bring a letter of authorization along to the interview.[56] Suspect can object to an interview being recorded, in such cases which should be recorded on the media, where the suspect does not want the media to record the objection, the media will be switched off with reasons given to the suspect. The suspect may later agree to have the interview recorded and questions will be put to the suspect. Interviews does not stop because there is a failure of an equipment and there is no replacement.

(i) Concluding the audio recorded interview under caution Suspects can clarify anything said earlier at the end of the interview and recording or add anything, notice of completion and announcement to switch of the recorder is then given to the person. The master tape/CD should be sealed, labeled and signed by the recorder, the suspect and any other persons present at the interview. Records of the fact that an audio recording took place, the time, duration, date and the identification number of the recording shall be kept on a notebook of recorded interview is required to be completed and kept by the recorder.

Lessons for the Nigerian Police from PACE

Under PACE, the rights of an accused person are referred to as continuing rights.[57]The law and its codes are well codified to regulate interviews and treatment of suspects during interrogations.

a) Interviews and interrogations of suspects are two separate processes and are not fused.

b) PACE tape recording is mandatory.

56 In effect that person is the company for the purposes of the interview under caution

57 PACE, Code C, 3.1Note for Guidance

c) As a result of heavy reliance on investigative interviewing [58]and less reliance on tactics, confession rates have been on the decline.[59]

d) S.78 of the law makes provision for court's discretion for the exclusion of an evidence which would have otherwise been admissible on the basis that it would be unfair to adduce it. This is a provision that is not available under the Evidence Act, 2011.

e) The rights of the mentally handicap and people with significant impairment in the area of intellect development and social functioning are provided for under Section 77 of PACE.

Code C& H[60] as amended is on right to have proceedings in a criminal trial interpreted and documents translated to an accused person's understanding with clarifications made to suspects by officers about the reasons for their detention and charge.

Codes E & F are amended to accommodate new provisions for the conduct and recording of voluntary interviews of suspects who are not under arrest. The responsibility of a sergeant towards interviews are also spelt out like giving authority, audio recording or not, cross referencing for the video recording of terrorists and security of master interview recordings so as to ensure consistency between Codes E and F and the new terrorism.

PACE and its codes has helped in reducing wrongful convictions unlike in the U.S.A. and other countries where minimization and psychological means are commonplace and wrongful convictions

---

58 PEACE (Participation and planning, engage and explain, account, closure and evaluate) simply to obtain as much information as possible.

59 Clarke C. and Milne R. 2001.National evaluation of the PEACE Investigative interviewing course, Home Office London Police Research Award Scheme, Report No. PRSA/149 Williamson, 2006.

60 Directive 2010/64/EU

are abound as a result of the high handed way of treatment of suspects at the pre-trial stage.

Caution is very significant under PACE interviews and non-compliance is regarded as an oppression and imposition of unjust burdens.[61] In Nigeria, through plethora of cases, non-administration of caution does not affect the voluntariness of statement.[62]

61 Caution exists under Section 10 (10.5) & Section 10 (8) of PACE ACT. There is special warning under the Criminal Justice and Public Order Act 1994, Section.36 & 37.

62 *State vs. Jimoh Salawu* (2011) 6-7 SC

REFERENCES

BOOKS

Adesiyan D.O 1996. An Accused Person's Rights in Nigeria Crimnal Law, Heinemann Educational Books Nigeria

Amnesty *International Document Nigeria. Time For Justice Accountability All index* Afr44/14/ 20001961.publication Ltd.

Anastasia Eruaga, Rights of silence of crime suspects is an unnecessary clog in the wheels of justice, www.nials.edu.ng last visited 20/1018

Aristotle 1959. *Politics*, London, Macmillan, iii 16;

DIAS R.W.M 1994.*Jurisprudence* 5th Ed. Delhi & U.K. Aditya Books Private Ltd. Butterworths

Dicey A.V. 1885. *Introduction to the study of the law of constitution,* 10th edition, London,

Basil Momodu, 2013. *Laws, rules and procedure of criminal investigation in Nigeria;* Evergreen Overseas Publications Ltd.

Bentham J. 1843. *The works of Jeremy Bentham,* 380.39, John Bowring, Ed. Edingburg. london. 11, 1818

Bittner, 1975. *The functions of the police in modern society for review of background factors, current practice and possible role models* (New York: Jason Aronson)

Bodede J. 2001. *Criminal evidence in Nigeria* 1st ed. Florence Lambard,

Cottrerrel R. 1992. *The Sociology of Law: An Introduction,* 2nd ed. Butterworths. 284.

Davies M. et.al 2005. *Criminal Justice; An Introduction to the Criminal Justice in England and Wales* 3rd Ed; Pearson Longman. Harlow, England.

David Dixon, 1997. *Law in Policing; Legal regulation and police practices*, Clarendon Press, oxford. E.O. Fakayode 1977. *The Nigerian criminal code companion,* Ethiope Publishing Corporation, Benin.

Elegido J.M. 1994. *Jurisprudence: A Textbook for Nigerian student's* Ed. Akinola Aguda, Spectrum Books ltd, Ibadan, Chap viii.

Finnis, J.F. 1980 *Natural law and Natural rights,* oxford 1980, Clarendon Press.

Fola Authur Worrey, 2000.*The prosecutor in public prosecutions* New /Ed.2000, Lagos State Ministry of Justice Law Review series.

Frank Agbedo, 2009. *Rights of suspects and Accused persons under Nigerian Criminal law* Crown Law publishers, 176

Hambally, D.U. 2012. *Practice and procedure of criminal litigation in Nigeria* Feat print and publish limited, Lagos.

Hart H.L.A. 1961, *The Concept of law.* Oxford, Portland.

Hewart, Lord 1925. *The new despotism,* London.

Holtham J. 2005 *Criminal litigation,* Guildford: college of law publishing. 2277

J.G. Riddal, 1999. *Jurisprudence* Butterworth, lexis Nexis 1st edition, rep., 2002. Derbyshire.

James Boswell 1970. *Life of Johnson* 685 R.W. Chapman ed. Oxford Univ. Press 1799.223.

John Austin 1954. *The province of jurisprudence determined.*

Kelsen, H. 1945. *General theory of law and state, translated by A. Wedberg* New York. Russell 1961. Kemi Rotimi 2001. *The police in a federal state: The Nigeria experience.* Ibadan College press ltd Klockars C. B 1985. *The idea of police.* United States.

Lai Oshitokunbo Oshisanya, 2008. *An almanac of contemporary judicial restatement with commentaries,* Spectrum Books Limited. Ibadan.

Marxism and legal pluralism 1 Australian Journal of law and Society Olatunbosun Adeniyi 2012. *Criminal justice in Nigeria,* Solerad Publishers.

Parker H. 1968. *The limits of the Criminal Sanction.* Stanford, CA: Stanford University Press.

Parker H. 1968. *The limits of the Criminal Sanction.* Stanford, CA: Stanford University Press. Roger Cottrerrel, 1992. *The sociology of law; An Introduction.* 2nd edition. Butterworths. Riddal J.G 1999. *Jurisprudence,* Butterworth, lexis Nexis 1st edition, rep. 2002. Derbyshire. Sebastine TAR. Hon (STV) 2012. *Law of evidence in Nigeria based on the Nigerian Evidence Act,* 2011

Vol. I Pearl Publishers.

Sidney A Afonja 2008. *Essential laws for the Nigeria police and other law Enforcement Agencies* Flocel publishers.

Simon, D. 1991. *Homicide: A year on the killing streets.* New York: Ivy Books.219

Stuntz W.J. 1989. The American Exclusionary Rule and Defendants' Changing Rights *Crim. L.*R 117-128.

Tamuno T.N. 1993. *Crime and security in the pre-colonial Nigeria in policing Nigeria past, present and future.* Malthouse Press Ltd.

Olatunbosun, A.2012 *Criminal Justice in Nigeria Solerad Publishers, Ibadan.*

Yemi Akinseye-George 2016. Issues on Criminal Justice Administration in Nigeria Eds. Adedeji Adekunle et.al *Prosecutorial Standards and the evaluation of Evidence under the Administration of Criminal Justice Act. 2015. Vol.95.*

JOURNALS

Ademola O.O 2013. Significance of an accused person's right to mandatory legal representation in Capital Offence, *Ibadan Bar Journal.* Vol.1, no.70-90 g

Agbonika John 2014. Delay in the Administration of Criminal Justice in Nigeria: issues from a Nigerian view point. *Journal of Law, policy and Globalization. Vol.26.130*

Ajomo M.A. et al, 1991. Human Rights and the Administration of Criminal Justice: Lagos Nigeria Institute of Advanced Legal Studies, N.I.A.L.S research studies series No. 1.121

Alex Stein, 2008. The Rights to silence helps the innocent – A Response to Critics, *Cardozo Law Review*, vol. 30; 3.

Andrew L.T 1991. Confessions and Corroboration: A comparative perspective, *The Criminal law report law Report,* 867-876

Ani, C.C. 2011. Reforms in the Nigerian criminal procedure laws: NIALS, *Journal of Criminal Law and Justice,* Vol. 1

Anne M. Coughlin, 2009. Interrogation stories; Victim blaming in the contemporary interrogation room is firmly entrenched in the contemporary in law in 2004 as in the early 1960 *Virginia Law Review* vol.95, Nov. no.7

Ashworth A. 2001. Criminal proceedings after the human Rights Acts. *The Criminal Law Review, 855-872*

Audi Jummai, 1999. Means of enforcing Human Rights accountability and democracy in Nigeria *A.B.U.L.J.* 6.

Awelle Lauretta, 2016. An examination of the Right of silence of a suspect under section 6 of the administration of Criminal Justice Act 2015 *Miyyetti Quarterly Law Review* vol.1 Issue 3

Babafemi Odunsi, 2011. Criminal law, disease control and HIV/AIDS contextualizing some challenges of the Nigerian criminal justice system' NIALS *Journal of Criminal Law And Justice,* Vol.1

Hirst J. 1993. Royal Commission Papers A Policing Perspective; Police Research Series, Paper 6, Eds. Gloria Laycock, Home office Police Research Group, London.

Baldwin J. 1993. Police interview techniques- establishing truth or proof? *British Journal of Criminology,* Vol. 33, Issue 3,325-352

Berger M. 1990. Legislating confession Law in Great Britain, A statutory approach to Police interrogation. *University of Michigan Journal of Law Reform.* Vol. 24. P1-64.

Cassel, P.G. 1996. Miranda's social cost: an empirical reassessment, *Northwestern University Law Review*, Vol. 90, No. 2, 1084-1124

Chin Tet Yung 2012. Criminal Procedure Code 2010. Confessions and Statements by Accused Persons Revisited 24 *SACLJ* 61.

Clarke, C. &Milne, R. 2001. National evaluation of the PEACE Investigative interviewing course, Home Office, London, Police *Research Award Scheme, Report No. PRSA/149*

Coughlin A.M. 2009. Interrogation stories; Victim blaming in the contemporary interrogation firmly entrenched in the contemporary Law in 2004 as in the early 1960 *Virginia Law Review,* vol.95, no.7, 1599- 1661

Daniel Lassiter et al. 1992.The potential for Bias in Videotaped confessions 1, *Journal of applied social psychology* vol.22 .issue 23, pages 1838-1851

David Wolchover et.al 1991. The questioning Code Revamped, The Crim L Review,232-249. deTurck & Miller, Training observers to detect deception, effects of self-monitoring and rehearsal,
Human Communication Research vol. 16 issue 4, 1990

Di Birch, 1989. The pace hots up: confessions and confusions under the 1984 Act; *The Criminal Law Review.*

Drizin & Leo, 2004. The problem of false confessions in the post DNA World, *North Carolina Law, Review*, Vol.82.

Drizin and Colgan, 2004. Tales from the Juvenile confession front: A guide to how standard police interrogation tactics can produced coerced and false confessions from juvenile suspects. Perspectives in law & psychology interrogative, confessions and entrapment Ed.s Daniel Lassiter V.20 New York, Kluvier Academic/ Plenum publishers.127- 162

Drizin S. A. 2004. The problem of false confessions in the post-DNA world. *North Carolina law review,* Vol. 82, 891-1007

Edwin Borchard 1932. *Convicting the innocent, and State indemnity for Errors of Criminal Justice ,* the Justice Institutions, New Haven , Yale University pp370- 371.

Ehighalu 2012. Nigeria issues on wrongful Convictions *University of Cincinnati law review.* Vol. 80 Review 1136. 15.4

Esa O. Onoja & T.S. Shankyula 2013. Refocusing the rules on admissibility of confessions in Nigeria to its constitutional Roots *Nigeria Bar Journal* Vol. 8, No. 1, Aug 2013, ISSN 0795-54

Fahey W. E. et al. 1987. False suspicion and the misperception of deceit. *British Journal of Social Psychology* 26, 41-46.

Famoye A. D., 2012. A historical survey of amalgamation of the Northern and Southern police departments of Nigeria in 1930 *European Scientific Journal* vol.8, no 18

Falana F. 2015. The Administration of Criminal Justice Act will ensure all law enforcement Agencies work together *This day Newspaper* Nigeria.

Fitzpartrick, P. 1983. Marxism and legal pluralism 1 *Australian Journal of law and Society.* Gilbert and Malone 1995. The Correspondence Bias, *Psychological Bulletin,* Vol.117, No.1, 21-38; Gregory N .O. 1994-1995. England limits the right to silence and moves towards an inquisitorial

system of justice, *Journal of Criminal Law and Criminology* 402 Vol.85, Issue 2

Gudjonsson G. H. *et. al.* 2008. False confessions: The relative importance of psychological, criminological and substance abuse variables; *Psychological crime & Law,* Vol.7, issue 3,275-289.

Gudjonsson G.H. *et. al.* 2007. Custodial interrogation what are the background factors associated with claims of false confession to police; *The Journal of Forensic psychiatry & psychology,* volume 18, issue 2.

Gudjonsson, G. H. 1992. *The psychology of interrogations, confessions and testimony. A Handbook* London: Wiley. Part 1, Chap.1

Hellen Fenwick 1993. Confessions, Recording rules and miscarriages of justice, a mistaken emphasis, Crim. L. R. 174-183.

Ibraheem, O. T. 2013 the Relevance of Confessions in Criminal Proceedings. *International Journal of Humanities and Social Science* Vol. 3 No. 21.

Inbau et.al 2001. *Criminal interrogation and confessions,* Aspen publishers 4th ed. *639*

Inbau F. E. *et. al.* 1986. *Criminal interrogation and confessions.*3rd ed. Baltimore. M.D Williams and wilkings. 364

Janet E. Stockdale 1993. Stockdale Management and supervision of police interviews. Great Britain; London. Police Research Group.

Jayne, B. C. 1986. The Psychological principles of criminal interrogation. *Criminal interrogation and confessions,* Eds. F Inbau, J. Reid, & J. Buckley 3rd Ed.

Leo, R. A. 1996a. Inside the interrogation room. *The Journal of Criminal Law and Criminology.Vol.88.* Jennifer T. Perillo and Saul M. Kassin, 2011. Conducted Inside Interrogation: The Lie, the Bluff and False Confessions, Cuny's John Jay College of Criminal Justice. *Law and Human Behavior,* Volume 35, Issue 4.

Chin. W.J.K, 2015. Criminal interrogation and the right to remain silent, a study of the Hong Kong customs service; *International Journal of Police Science & Management Volume* 11 number 2.A 2015

Ibraheem, O.T,2013. The relevance of confessions in criminal proceedings. *International Journal of Humanities and Social Science* 3.21:Special issue- December 291-300 at 291.

Karl Roberts, 2012. Police interviewing of criminal suspects: A historical perspective; *internet journal of Criminology, 1-17,* retrieved from www.cbc.ca; 31st August 2016

Kassin & Fong, 2002. CT I'm innocent effects of training on judgments of truth and deception in the interrogation room, *law Hum Behave*, 26-133-58

Kassin & Neumann, 1997. Power of confession evidence and experimental test of the fundamental difference hypothesis randomized controlled trial. *Law hum Behav,* Oct.; 21 (5) 469 -84

Kassin & Sukel, 1997. Coerced Confessions and the jury, *Law Hum Behav.* 21-27-46

Kassin S. et al. 2009. Police – induced confessions, Risk factors and recommendation factors, *Law and Human Behav.* 2010.

Kassin S.M et.al. 2003. *The psychology of confessions: A review of the literature and issues of psychological science in the public Interest.*Vol.5. Sage Publisher.

Kassin S.M. 2011. Current directions in Psychological Science. *Journal of applied research in memory and cognition,* 2(1) Vol. 20

Kassin S.M. et al 1999. I'm Innocent! Effects of Training on Judgments of Truth and Deception in the Interrogation Room. Law and Human Behav. vol. 23, No. 5 499-516

Kassin S.M. 2006. A critical appraisal of modern police interrogations (from investigative interviewing, rights, research, regulation, Tom Williamson, Ed. Interviewing, Rights, Research regulation.pp.207-228, Devon, United Kingdom, William Publishing.

Kassins & Gudjonssin, 2004. The psychology of confession; a review of the literature and issues. *The psychological science in the public interest.* Nov 1.5(2): 33-67

Lassiter G.D. et.al. 1986. Videotaped confession: The impact of Camera point of view on judgments of coercion. *Journal of Applied Social Psychology.* Vol. 16, (3) 268-278

Lassiter G.D.et. al. 2006. Videotaped confessions: Panacea or Pandora's Box. *Law& Policy Journal,* Vol. 28, Issue 2, 192-210

Olanrewaju O. *et. al.* 2016. An appraisal of the attitude of courts to the ACJA. *Miyyetti Quarterly law review* Vol. 1 (issue 1).

Leo & Ofshe, 1998. The consequences of false confessions; Deprivations of liberty and miscarriages of justice in the age of psychology *Journal of Criminal Law and criminology* Vol. 88. Issue 2,429-496.

Leo and Liu, 2009. What do potential jurors know about police interrogation techniques and false confessions *Behavioural Sciences& the law* 27 (3) 381-99.

Leo Ofshe, 2001. The truth about false confessions and advocacy scholarship, *Criminal law Bulletin* Vol. 37, 78; Sage journals.

Leo, R. A. 1996a. Inside the interrogation room. The Journal of Criminal Law and criminology Vol. 88.

Max Guyll, et al. 2013. Law and Human Behavior, Innocence and Resisting Confession during Interrogation: Effects on Physiologic Activity, *Law and Human Behavior,*

Meissner & Kassin, 2002. He is guilty, investigator bias in judgments of truth and deception *Law and Human Behaviour,* Volume 26, Issue 5.

Meissner, et.al. 2012. *Techniques and controversies in the interrogation of suspects: The artful practice versus the scientific study Psychological science in the courtroom: controversies and consensus. The importance of a laboratory science for improving the diagonistic value of confession evidence,*Guilford press 2009

Mirfield P. 1984. The future of the law of confessions *Crim. L.R.* 63.

Moore E. & C. Lindsay Fitzsimmons, justice imperiled 2011: Confessions and the reid technique" *Criminal Law Quarterly,* Vol.57.

Odunsi B. 2015.Criminal Law, Disease Control and HIV/AIDS Contextualizing some challenges of the Nigerian Criminal Justice System. *NIALS Journal of Criminal Law and Justice,* Vol. 1. 1-29

Ochem C.M.2011. The Relevance of confessional statement in Criminal Proceedings in Nigeria, *Igbinedion University Journal of Jurisprudence & Public Law* Vol.1, no.2,2011 p.23

Ofshe & Leo 1997. The decision to confess falsely; Rational The consequences of false confessions: Deprivations of liberty and miscarriages of Justice in the age of psychological interrogation, *The journal of criminal , Law & criminology,* Vol. 88,No 2.

Oghi F.E. 2013. Reflections of Africa's security situation (2013): An examination of Nigeria. Obior et.al 2002. Legalism, popular Agency and Voices of suffering The Nigerian National

Human Rights Commission in context in Police Force *Human Quarterly,* Vol.24 (August)
N0.3,

Olanrewaju O. (SAN) et.al. 2016. An appraisal of the attitude of the Courts to the administration of Criminal Justice Act 2015 *Miyyetti quarterly Law review,* Vol. 1, (issue 1)

O'Sullivan M et al. 1991. Who can catch a liar? America Psychologist, 46

Okeshola, F.B.2013. Human rights abuse by Nigerian police in four selected states and the federal Capital Territory, Abuja, *British Journal of Arts and Social sciences*Vol.13. no.11 Ibraheem, O.T. 2013. The relevance of confessions in criminal proceedings. *International Journal of Humanities and Social Science* 3.21: (Special issue- December) 291-300 at 291.

Povey, D. et al 2009. Home office Statistical Bulletin: Police powers and procedures England and Wales 2007/08 London: HMSO

Preferser S. 1960. *Pretrial procedure of the accused, a comparative study*, London Steweus & Son (1966) Reid, & J. Buckley. *Criminal interrogation and confessions* 3rd Ed.

Reitz J. 1998. How to do comparative law, *The American journal of Comparative Law,* vol.46, no. 4, August. 1994.

Remington M.J. 1960. Law Relating to on the street detention ,Questioning and Frisking of suspected persons and Police Arrest Privileges in General ,51 *J Crim. L. Criminology & Police Sc.*

Richard Leo 2009. False confession, causes, consequences and implications. *The journal of the American Academy and the law,* law 37,322-43;

Richard Leo, 2009.Confession evidence, 67-94, 77 *The psychology of Evidence and Trial procedure,* Kassin & Wrightsman Eds. Beverly Hills Sage Publications.67-94,77

Ronald C. H. & Martin K. 2013. Errors occur everywhere but not at the same frequency. The role of procedural systems in Wrongful convictions and Miscarriages of justice; Causes and remedies in North American and European Criminal Justice ed. chapter 4 University Zurich.

Routledge T.& Francis Group, New York and London; Cleen Foundation page 23 6/29/2005. Sanders, Bridge, Mulvaney and Crozier, 1990. Advice and Assistance at Police stations and the 24 hour Duty solicitor scheme, *Crim, l. Review*495-509

Kassin S.M.& Gudjosson, G.H. 2004. The psychology of Interrogation and confessions; A Review of the literature and issues of psychological science in the Public.5,35-39

Sigurdsson & Gudjonsson (1996a). The psychological characteristics of false confessions: a study among Icelandic prisons; Journal, Psychology, crime & Law, vol. 10, issue 2

Sigurdsson et.al Gudjonsson, 2001. The relative importance of psychological, criminological and substance abuse variables; *Psychology Crime and law* 1-4

Stefan A.R 1949. Law making and Legislative Precedent in America Legal History,33

Suzzie O. O.*et.al.* 2016. Recording of statements made by suspects , A review of S.17 of the Administration of Criminal justice, 2015; *Issues on criminal justice administration in Nigeria,* Eds. Adedeji Adekunle et.al Chap.6, pp122-143 NIALS Lagos .*Minn. L. Review*103,118

Stephenson, G.M. & Moston, S.J. 1994. Police interrogation. Psychology, Crime & Law, Vol. 1 Stephenson G. M. & Moston S.J. 1993. Attitudes and assumptions of Police officers when questioning criminal suspects. Issues in Criminological and legal psychology, Crime & Law, No.18

Steven G., 1990. The Right to silence, a review of the current debate 53 *Modern law review,* 709; J.D Jackson.

Stuntz W.J. 1989. The American Exclusionary Rule and Defendants' Changing Rights *Crim. L.R* 117-128.

Soukara B. *et. al.,* 2009.What really happens in police interviews with suspects: tactics and confessions psychology; *crime & Law* vol.15 no.66.

Tom B.*et. al.* (2000). The rights of silence, The Impacts of the Criminal Justice and Public Act, 1994 Home office Research study.

Vrij, A. 1994. The impact of information and setting on detection of deception by police detectives. *Journal of Nonverbal Behavior*, 18.

Wald, Ayres, Hess, Schantz, & Whitebread 1967. Interrogations in new Haven: The impact of Miranda. Vol. 76 *Yale law Journal.*

Warren C.J Irving and Hilgendorf, Research study no: 1 Royal Commission on criminal procedure. Wickersham Commission Report, 1931.*The American Journal of Police Science* Vol. 2, No 4. Akinseye-George Y. 2016. Issues on Criminal Justice Administration in Nigeria, Eds. Adedeji

Adekunle et.al Prosecutorial Standards and the evaluation of Evidence under the Administration of Criminal Justice Act. 2015.

Zuckerman M., DePaulo, B. M., & Rosenthal, R. 1981. Verbal and nonverbal communication of deception. Advances in Experimental Social Psychology, 14.

Zulawski, D. E. & Wicklander, D. E. 1993. Practical aspects of interview and interrogation.
Oxford.

CONFERENCE PAPERS

Richard Rogers Ph.D (2011); Rights to Remain Silent not understood by many suspects, a paper delivered at the 119th convention of the American psychologist Association. Retrieved from American psychological Association Site on 2/2/2016.

CONVENTIONS

European Convention on Human Rights. (1953)
Convention against Torture and other Cruel, Inhuman or Degrading Treatment or Punishment (1984)
The African Charter on Human and Peoples Rights (1986)
International Covenant on Civil and Political Rights (1966),
Universal Declaration of Human Rights (1948).

NEWSPAPERS

Heather Mills; Tougher policies at helping Victims of Crime, The Independent (London)
Oct,6,1993 at 25, editorial.
The Guardian, feb.11, 2015
The Nation, Law. Tuesday, September 27, 2016
Femi Falana: The Administration of Criminal Justice Act will ensure all law enforcement Agencies work together; This day Newspaper Nigeria, 9 November ,2015

INTERNET

(http://www.courttv.com/trials/tuite/) last visited on 22/9/18 (http://www.reid.com/service-bai-interview.html). Last visited April 2001. Http://www.ngguardian news.com 2015/0823/9/18 (http://www.reid.com/service-bai-interview.html). Last visited 23/9/18 False Confessions.org. Visited 18/11/17.

Innocence Staff; The innocence project, 2018, a record year in exoneration. Retrieved on 11th of November, 2017 from https://www.innocenceproject last visited 15/11/17.

www.pulse.ng/ news/ local Bola-Ige, visited 1/5/2018

Amnesty International; Nigeria Human Rights Agenda; 31st May 2019, Index no. AFR 44/ 0431/ 2019 Http.//www.amnesty.ng/en/countries/africa/nigeria/right-riteria, visited 18/11/17.

https://www.innocenceproject (last visited 15/11/17)). https://www.innocenceproject.org.visited 10/September, 2018. Arizona vs. Fulminate 499, US 279 296 (1991) https://twiter.com/innocence. 18/11/17. https://www.innocenceproject (last visited 15/11/17)).

Robinson, M., What is Social Justice? QEP Global Learning, department of Government of Government and Justice studies, Appalachian State University. Retrieved September 20, 2015,http://gis.appstate.edu/social-justice-and-human-rights/what-social-justice.

Stephen Gaskell. 2015,*Psycholegal Assesments inc.False Confession Research;* Retrieved Oct. 20th 2018 from https://psycholegalassesments.com/false -confession-research/

INDEX

Act of Parliament, 34 Administration of criminal Justice Act, ix
Administrative workload, 65
Adversarial style, 51, 78
Aggressive techniques, 36, 60
Amendments, 159
Americal constitution, 71, 84
Anti-Torture Act, 2017, 133
Apprehension, 45

Behavioral analysis, 63
Bluff techniques, 46

Civil procedure, 24
Civil Society Organization, 118 Coerced confession, 25, 54
– false confession, 32 Coercion, 25
Criminal Justice Act, 1998, 72 Criminal Justice Act, 2003, 72 Criminal Justice and police Act, 2001, 72
Criminal justice system, 50, 55 Criminal trials, 24, 29 Cross examination, 103
Culpability, ix
Custodial interrogation, 29

Discretion, 63
Doctrine of entrapment, 27 English Humn Rights Acts, 104

English law, 35, 79

Ethical ways, 33
Evidence Act, ix, 23, 26, 30, 31, 123, 147
Eye witness, 24
False confession, 41, 42, 43
False confessor, 48
False evidence, 66
Field experiments, 51
Fingerprint database, 81, 95
Forensic investigation, 81

Guilty feeling, 44

Human Rights Act of 1998, 79

Independent facts, 26
Inducement, 147
Investigating Police Officer, 35, 131
Involuntary statement, ix

Judicial statement, 25

Law enforcement officers, 56 Local language, 110

Ministry of Justice, 99
Miscarriage of justice, 35
National human Right Commission, 134
National Insurance Number, 162 Nigerian Law reform Commission (NLRC), 91

PACE code, 34

Police and Criminal evidence Act, 1984, 81
Police and criminal Evidence Act, 25, 34
Police and justice Act 2006, 72
Police Commissioner, 73
Police investigation , 24
Police reform Act, 2002, 72
Prejudiced source, 56
Psychological stress, 59
Psychological tactics, 114
Public Compliants Commission, 107

Randomized trial, 51
Real trial, 57
Roman law, 23

Self-incriminating statements, 65

Terrorism, 159
Terrorist Act, 140
The Reid Technique, 61, 93
Third degree method, 42
Torture Convention, 140

www.ingramcontent.com/pod-product-compliance
Lightning Source LLC
LaVergne TN
LVHW080815170826
845678LV00011B/2011

* 9 7 9 8 8 4 9 5 6 0 1 5 1 *